SIMPLE CROCHET FOR CHERISHED BABIES

SIMPLE CROCHET FOR CHERISHED BABIES

By Jane Davis

LARK BOOKS

A Division of Sterling Publishing Co., Inc.
New York

EDITOR
Joanne O'Sullivan

ART DIRECTOR
Dana Irwin

COVER DESIGN
Barbara Zaretsky

BOOK DESIGN
Key Associates Design

PHOTOGRAPHY
Sandra Stambaugh

ILLUSTRATIONS
Orrin Lundgren

EDITORIAL ASSISTANCE
Anne Wolff Hollyfield
Delores Gosnell

PRODUCTION ASSISTANCE
Hannes Charen

Library of Congress Cataloging-in-Publication Data
Davis, Jane, 1959-
    Simple crochet for cherished babies / by Jane Davis
        p. cm.
    ISBN 1-57990-417-3 (Paperback)
    1. Crocheting--Patterns. 2. Infants' clothing. I. Title.

TT825.D385 2003
746.43'40432--dc21   2003004390

10 9 8 7 6 5 4 3 2 1

Published by Lark Books, a division of
Sterling Publishing Co., Inc.
387 Park Avenue South, New York, N.Y. 10016

© 2003, Jane Davis

Distributed in Canada by Sterling Publishing,
c/o Canadian Manda Group, 165 Dufferin Street
Toronto, Ontario, Canada M6K 3H6

Distributed in the U.K. by: Guild of Master Craftsman Publications Ltd.
Castle Place, 166 High Street, Lewes, East Sussex, England BN7 1XU
Tel: (+ 44) 1273 477374, Fax: (+ 44) 1273 478606
Email: pubs@thegmcgroup.com, Web: www.gmcpublications.com

Distributed in Australia by Capricorn Link (Australia) Pty Ltd.,
P.O. Box 704, Windsor, NSW 2756 Australia

If you have questions or comments about this book, please contact:
Lark Books • 67 Broadway • Asheville, NC 28801 • (828) 253-0467

Manufactured in China

ISBN 1-57990-417-3   1-57990-740-7

For information about custom editions, special sales, premium and
corporate purchases, please contact Sterling Special Sales Department
at 800-805-5489 or specialsales@sterlingpub.com.

CONTENTS

INTRODUCTION

When I was pregnant with my first son, one of my co-workers gave me a crocheted baby blanket she had made herself. I was touched that she had spent the time to make this beautiful, yet practical, treasure for my baby. Every time I pulled the blanket to cover my son when he was cold, I thought of her and the time and effort she had put into making her gift. When he got too big for the crib, I carefully folded the blanket and packed it away so I can give it to him when he has a family of his own. I hope the projects in this book will be as meaningful for your friends and family as that blanket was for me. Whether they are made by a grandmother to a new grand-daughter-to-be, by an expectant mother as she waits for her baby, or by a friend who wants to show she cares, they are meant to be more than just a gift—they are lasting symbols of love and friendship.

With basic crochet skills, you'll find that most of the projects in this book prove easy to make (there are a few challenging items included as well!). The designs are fun and interesting, with a classic feel. Many of the projects are simple struc-tures made from rectangles, squares, and tubes, worked in easy, allover stitch repeats. You'll be familiar with the basic crochet stitches used to make them, and with the added instructions and

illustrations for the specialty stitches used to pull everything together, you'll be able to create something special for your favorite little one.

The finishing touches make these projects exciting. From a ribbon-edged border or a bit of embroidery to a unique closure or stitch detail, the little extras make your project truly special. You can adapt the ideas and designs to make your own unique creations. I hope you'll seek out antique ribbons or closures, or recycle such items from old clothing that has meaning to you, such as a button from a favorite old blouse. Sometimes just the addition of a special touch is all you need to make an heirloom piece.

The colors used for the projects were chosen for their timeless appeal. Soft muted shades with names like "buttermilk" and "rose petal" reflect the feelings of caring for a baby and look really wonderful against a baby's delicate skin.

For ease in construction (and since babies come in all different shapes and sizes), you'll find sizing information to help make your gift in a range of sizes. I think using quality yarn is important too, so I've included a section on yarn choice and care instructions for delicate crocheted items.

Whether you choose to make a simple toy or a blanket and pillow set, I hope you'll enjoy making these projects as much as I did.

GETTING STARTED

Specialty Stitches

Although most of the crochet stitches for these projects are basic single crochet, half-double crochet, and double crochet, there are some specialty stitches which you may not know. The following stitches are found in projects throughout the book.

ABBREVIATIONS

beg: BEGIN/BEGINNING

bpdc: BACK-POST DOUBLE CROCHET

ch: CHAIN

ch sp: CHAIN SPACE

dc: DOUBLE CROCHET

ea: EACH

fpdc: FRONT-POST DOUBLE CROCHET

hdc: HALF-DOUBLE CROCHET

hk: HOOK

htr: HALF-TRIPLE CROCHET

inc: INCREASE

lp(s): LOOP(S)

patt: PATTERN

rep(s): REPEAT(S)

sc: SINGLE CROCHET

sk #: SKIP ONE OR MORE STITCHES UNLESS STATED OTHERWISE

sl st(s): SLIP STITCH(ES)

st(s): STITCH(ES)

tog: TOGETHER

tr: TRIPLE CROCHET

yo: YARN OVER

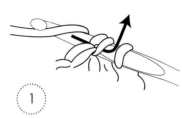
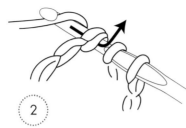

CLUSTERS

For these stitches, you do all but the last yo and pull through of each stitch until the very end. Using clusters, all your stitches end with one yo and pull through, decreasing the group of stitches to one.

2-sc cluster

Insert hk in next st, yo, pull through st, insert hk in next st, yo pull through st, yo, pull through all lps on hk (see figures 1, 2, 3).
(Used in: Turtle, Rascal Hat)

3-dc cluster

[Yo, insert hk in next st, yo, pull through st, yo, pull through 2 lps on hk] 3 times, yo, pull through all lps on hk (see figure 4).
(Used in: Tumbling Blocks Blanket)

4-dc cluster

[Yo, insert hk in next st, yo, pull through st, yo, pull through 2 lps on hk] 4 times, yo, pull through all lps on hk (see figure 5).
(Used in: Tumbling Blocks Blanket, Bargello Pillow)

5-dc cluster

[Yo, insert hk in next st, yo, pull through st, yo, pull through 2 lps on hk] 5 times, yo, pull through all lps on hk (see figure 6).
(Used in: Wild Rose Blanket)

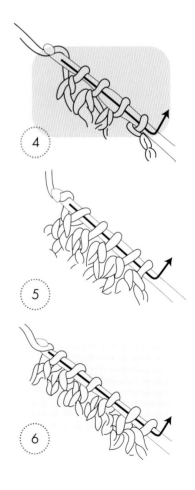

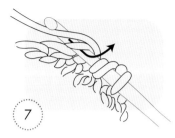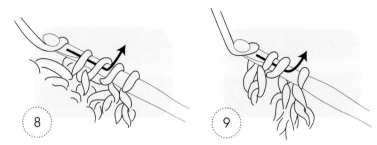

The following stitches are used to make the heel for the booties and footed outfits.

2-tr cluster

[Yo twice, insert hk in next st, yo, pull through st, yo, pull through 2 lps, yo, pull through 2 lps] 2 times. There will be 3 lps on the hk. Yo, pull through all lps (see figure 7, figure 8, figure 9).
(Used in: Buttercup Footies, Dainty Slippers, Dusty Rose Booties, Little Boy Blue Booties)

3-tr cluster

[Yo twice, insert hk in next st, yo hk, pull through st, yo, pull through 2 lps, yo, pull through 2 lps] 3 times. There will be 4 lps on the hk. Yo, pull through all lps (see figures 7, 8, 9 above).
(Used in: Buttercup Footies, Dusty Rose Booties, Dainty Slippers, Little Boy Blue Booties)

SHELLS

These are stitch groups in which you make three or more stitches in the same location, forming a shell shape. They can be used for increases, turning corners, and for the decorative shell shapes in patterns, especially as a final edging to finish a design. The instructions state how many and what kind of stitches to make (and in what stitch). If there is a following row, this group of stitches will be referred to as a shell.

US AND EUROPEAN EQUIVALENTS

Crochet terminology is different in the US than in European countries. All of the instructions in this book are written using US standards. The following table shows the equivalent European terms.

US Terms	European Equivalents
slip stitch (sl st)	single crochet
single crochet (sc)	double crochet
half-double crochet (hdc)	half-treble crochet
double crochet (dc)	treble crochet
triple crochet (tr)	double treble

CROCHET TERMS

Crochet is an evolving craft with many variations. Instructions for crocheting are as varied as the technique. Following are guidelines to help you understand my methods of writing these instructions.

ASTERISKS (*). Repeat the instructions between asterisks as indicated.

BRACKETS []. Work the instructions within the brackets the number of times indicated after the brackets.

FOUNDATION. The beginning chain, into which the first row is crocheted. I usually begin the first row by crocheting under the two top threads of the chain unless I'm working around both sides of the foundation chain (as in the booties on pages 47, 73, and 80). Unless the instructions specify, you can crochet under both threads or just one half of the foundation stitch for the first row.

PARENTHESES (). Parentheses are used in the same way as brackets. Parentheses enclose instructions which contain a section repeated in brackets. This helps to distinguish one set of repeats from another. Parentheses are also used to indicate variations in the instructions based on different sizes.

PLACE MARKER. Indicates where to slip an open-ended marker into the completed stitch, marking the beginning or the end of the round.

STEP-UP or TURNING CHAIN. The chain or chains used at the beginning of a new row to raise the level of work to the height of the new row you are about to begin. For most projects in this book, the turning chain is not counted as a stitch. Look at the "Pattern Notes" at the beginning of each pattern to determine if the turning chain is counted. On the first row (and all rows) I always list the turning chain at the beginning of the row, rather than as part of the foundation stitches or at the end of the row. This makes sense to me, since it really is a part of the current row, and not the row before.

WORK EVEN. Continue each row in pattern, with no increases or decreases.

OTHER STITCHES

Fpdc and Bpdc

These stitches are basically the same—one is worked from the front of the work and the other is worked from the back. The stitch causes the work to be raised or recessed, opening up many possibilities for texture such as cabling and basketweave textures.
(Used in: Winter Wonderland Hat and Cable Sweater)

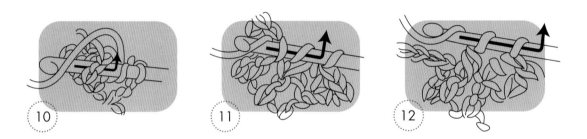

Front-Post Double Crochet

Work double crochet by first inserting the hook behind the vertical section, or post, of the stitch rather than the chain at the top of the stitch. Complete the stitch as usual (see figure 10, figure 11, figure 12).

Back-Post Double Crochet

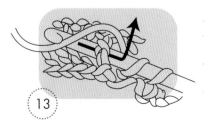

Work double crochet by first inserting the hk from the back side of the work, around the vertical section, or post, of the st rather than the ch at the top of the st. Complete the st as usual (see figure 13).

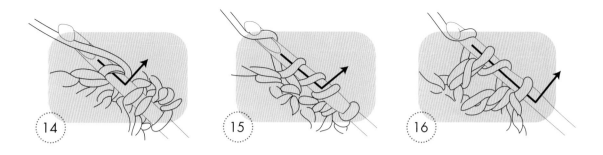

14 15 16

Htr: Half-Triple Crochet

This stitch can be worked in two ways. This is the way I made the stitch for the projects in this book: Yo hk twice, insert hk in next st, yo hk, pull through st, yo hk, pull through 2 lps on hk, yo hk, pull through remaining 3 lps on hk (see figure 14, figure 15, figure 16).

(Used in: Wild Rose Blanket)

EMBELLISHMENTS

Many of the projects use embroidery to embellish the finished items or for assembly. Following are the stitches you will need to know.

Note: Always be careful with embellishments on baby clothes, keeping in mind the baby's safety. Check that items are sewn firmly onto the garment, toy, or blanket, and check them often when in use to make sure that they haven't become loose.

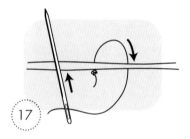

17

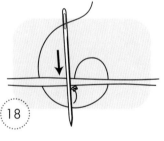

18

Back Stitch

This stitch is good for reinforcement. Insert the needle, bring out a stitch behind, then insert the needle a stitch ahead (see figures 17, 18, 19).

(Used in: Buttercup Footies, Bargello Pillow)

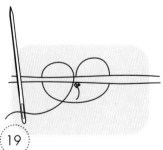

19

lps on hk] 5 times, yo, pull through all lps on hk (see figure 6).
(Used in: Wild Rose Blanket)
The following stitches are used to make the heel for the booties and footed outfits.

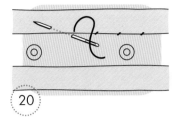

2-tr cluster

[Yo twice, insert hk in next st, yo, pull through st, yo, pull through 2 lps, yo, pull through 2 lps] 2 times. There will be 3 lps on the hk. Yo, pull through all lps (see figure 7, figure 8, figure 9).
(Used in: Buttercup Footies, Dainty Slippers, Dusty Rose Booties, Little Boy Blue Booties)

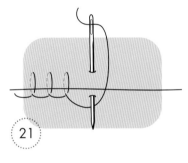

3-tr cluster

CROCHET HOOK SIZES

Use the following table as a guide for the hook sizes used in this book. Keep in mind that sizes may vary slightly from company to company and between letter name and metric size. Make your project with whichever size hook gives you the intended gauge.

U.S.	Metric	U.K.
D/3	3.25	10
E/4	3.5	9
F/5	3.75	8
G/6	4	7
H/8	5	6
I /9	5.5	5
J/10	6	4
K/10.5	6.5	2

14

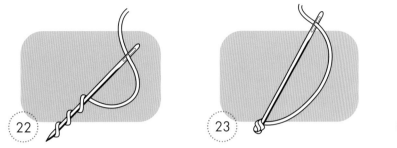

22

23

24

[Yo twice, insert hk in next st, yo hk, pull through st, yo, pull through 2 lps, yo, pull through 2 lps] 3 times. There will be 4 lps on the hk. Yo, pull through all lps (see figures 7, 8, 9 above). *(Used in: Buttercup Footies, Dusty Rose Booties, Dainty Slippers, Little Boy Blue Booties)*

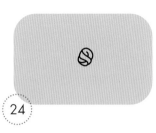

25

SHELLS

These are stitch groups in which you make three or more stitches in the same location, forming a shell shape. They can be used for increases, turning corners, and for the decorative shell shapes in patterns, especially as a final edging to finish a design. The instructions state how many and what kind of stitches to make (and in what stitch). If there is a following row, this group of stitches will be referred to as a shell.

Htr: Half-Triple Crochet

This stitch can be worked in two ways. This is the way I made the stitch for the projects in this book: Yo hk twice, insert hk in

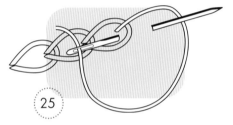

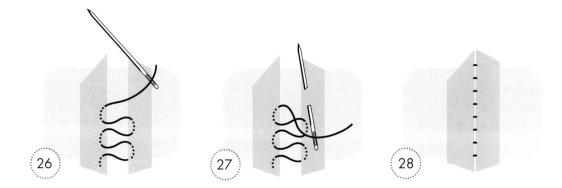

Kitchener stitch

This is the basic stitch used to assemble all the projects unless stated otherwise. When sewing two seams together, take a small vertical stitch, in and out, on one side on the right side of the crochetwork, then make another vertical stitch directly across on the edge of the other piece. Pull snugly so the stitches disappear and the two pieces of crochetwork pull together (see figures 26, 27, 28).

Satin Stitch

On the right side of your work, bring the needle up at the lower edge of the area you want to cover, and insert the needle directly across the area. Make each stitch touching the previous one (see figure 29). *(Used in: Wooly Lamb)*

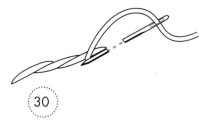

Stem Stitch

This stitch is the opposite of back stitch. You take a long stitch on the top of the fabric in one direction, and a short stitch on the back side of the fabric in the other direction (see figure 30). *(Used in: Turtle, Wild Rose Blanket)*

Straight Stitch

Tie a knot and pass up through the back of the fabric where you want the stitch to begin. Pass down through the top of the fabric where you want the stitch to end and back up where you want the next stitch to begin (see figure 31). *(Used in: Turtle, Wooly Lamb)*

BABY SIZING TABLE

As with all garment construction, sizes vary from person to person, so be sure to check that the size you're making will be appropriate for the baby. If the item is a gift and you can't be sure of the size, make the item a size or two larger. If it's too big, there's room to grow into it. If it's too small, it may never to be worn at all.

The following chart of baby measurements was used to calculate sizes for projects in this book. Finished sizes are usually larger, allowing for ease of fit. Hats are the same size or smaller so they will stretch to fit.

Description	Newborn	1 to 3 Months	3 to 6 Months	6 to 9 Months	9 to 12 Months
Head circumference	14 in. (35.6 cm)	16 in. (40.6 cm)	17 in. (43.2 cm)	18 in. (45.7 cm)	19 in. (48.3 cm)
Chest circumference	14 in. (35.6 cm)	16 in. (40.6 cm)	18 in. (45.7 cm)	19 in. (48.3 cm)	20 in. (50.8 cm)
Back of neck to hip length	8 in. (20.3 cm)	9 in. (22.9 cm)	10 in. (25.4 cm)	11 in. (27.9 cm)	12 in. (30.5 cm)
Waist to ankle length	12 in. (30.5 cm)	13 in. (33 cm)	14 in. (35.6 cm)	15 in. (38.1 cm)	16 in. (40.6 cm)
Crotch to ankle length	6 in. (15.2 cm)	7 in. (17.8 cm)	8 in. (20.3 cm)	9 in. (22.9 cm)	10 in. (25.4 cm)
Sleeve length	8 in. (20.3 cm)	9 in. (22.9 cm)	11 in. (27.9 cm)	13 in. (33 cm)	14 in. (35.6 cm)

YARN CONSIDERATIONS

Using a quality yarn is important for the success of your baby crochet project. Even if an outfit will be worn only once for a picture, it may be kept for years to take out again for the next little one, or shown to the one who's now all grown up. I have used mostly wools, because I like them and the colors are beautifully subtle. If you are worried about itchiness, look for softer yarns, though beware. Acrylics can be just as itchy as wool. Some wools, especially merino, extra-fine merino, or alpaca, can be ever-so-soft.

Caring for Hand-Crocheted Baby Items

The time spent to create a special garment, toy, or blanket for a baby makes the item something special, so special care should be taken to keep the item clean.

By nature, babies love to explore with their little fingers, feet, and mouths. This leads to dirt, and dirt leads to germs. Since yarn absorbs germs easily, crocheted baby items need to be cleaned frequently so babies don't get sick. But yarn isn't always easy to clean—it's easily abraded and isn't always machine washable.

If the yarn you use is machine washable, you should first make a small swatch in the pattern stitch you will be using and put it through the washer and dryer to see how it holds up. If you use yarn that's not machine washable, I recommend hand washing in a mild soap made especially for hand knits or hand crochet work, or using a mild dish soap. Soak the item in lukewarm water with a small amount of soap. Agitate it gently by hand, spending a little more time with any dirt spots or areas you know are soiled. Rinse in clean lukewarm water and squeeze out excess water without twisting or wringing the yarn. Finally, remove as much moisture as possible by rolling the crochetwork in a dry towel. You may need to do this several times with clean dry towels to get most of the water out of the yarn. Lay the piece flat in a warm dry place to finish drying.

Yarn Substitutions

I recommend using the yarn used in the sample project for the most successful results. However, you may wish to use a different yarn for many reasons. Sometimes you'll just have to use a particular yarn because it's just the right color. You may prefer synthetics for easy care. Hypoallergenic yarn can be softer on the skin. When substituting yarn, always first try yarn in the same weight as the sample project yarn, and as always, make a test swatch in the pattern stitch or gauge stitch to make sure the yarn will work up the same. Even yarn of the same weight may work up differently if it's a different type of yarn.

PRETTY IN PINK SUNDRESS
and Sun Hat

SKILL LEVEL
Intermediate

This adorable dress and matching hat make any warm-weather outing a special occasion. Soft pink cotton yarn wears well and shows off the delicate crochet pattern. The easy-to-make hat protects Baby's delicate skin from the sun.

Stitches Used

single crochet (sc)
double crochet (dc)

You Will Need

4 skeins (each 125 yards [115m]) of fingering-weight cotton yarn in pale pink

Size E hook

Tapestry needle

2³/₈-inch (9.5 mm) buttons or flower-shaped beads

Sewing needle and thread

Pattern Notes

To decrease at the beginning of a row on the yoke, skip the first st, continue in patt. Step up is not counted as a stitch in this project.

To decrease at the end of a row on the yoke, work to the last 2 sts in the row, hk through the first st, yo the hk and pull through st (two lps on hk), hk through the last st, yo the hk and pull through st (three lps on hk), yo the hk, and pull through all lps on hk (one lp left on hk).

Yoke Back

Foundation: Ch 31 (34, 37, 40, 43).

Row 1: Ch 1, sc in 2nd ch from hk and ea ch across, turn.

Rows 2 to 5: Ch 1, dec 1, sc in ea st to last 2 sts, dec 1, turn (23, 26, 29, 32, 35 sts).

Work even for 11 (11, 11, 13, 13) rows.

Right Back Shoulder

Row 1: Ch 1, 10 (10, 11, 11, 12) sc, dec 1, turn (11, 11, 12, 12, 13 sts).

Dec 1 st at the neckline edge of ea row and work the armhole edge even for 4 (4, 5, 6, 6) rows (7 sts).

Work 1 row even.

Left Back Shoulder

Attach a new length of yarn to the top row of the yoke piece on the 12th (12th, 13th, 13th, 14th) st from the left side.

Row 1: Ch 1, 11 (11, 12, 12, 13) sc to end, turn (11, 11, 12, 12, 13 sts).

Finish as for right back shoulder.

Yoke Front and Shoulders

Work the same as for the yoke back and shoulders, except for the following:

After row 5 on the yoke, work only 7 (7, 7, 9, 9) rows even before beginning shoulder sections.

On the shoulder sections, instead of working 1 row even at the end, work a total of 5 rows even.

On the left front shoulder make the buttonhole placket (following).

Buttonhole Placket

Row 1: Ch 1, 7 sc, turn.

Row 2: Ch 1, sc, ch 2, sk 2, sc, ch 2, sk 2, sc in last st, turn.

Row 3: Ch 1, sc, 2 sc in ch sp, sc, 2 sc in ch sp, sc in last st.

Weave in end.

Finished Measurements

Size	Width at Base of Yoke	Length from shoulder to skirt edge	Skirt Length	Skirt Circumference
Newborn	6 in. (15.2 cm)	10 in. (25.4 cm)	7 in. (17.8 cm)	23 in. (58.4 cm)
1 to 3 months	6 1/2 in. (16.5 cm)	10 3/4 in. (27.3 cm)	7 3/4 in. (19.6 cm)	26 in. (66 cm)
3 to 6 months	7 in. (17.8 cm)	11 1/2 in. (29.2 cm)	8 in. (20.3 cm)	28 in. (71.1 cm)
6 to 9 months	7 1/2 in. (19 cm)	12 1/2 in. (31.8 cm)	8 1/2 in. (21.6 cm)	30 in. (76.2 cm)
9 to 12 months	8 in. (20.3 cm)	13 1/2 in. (34.3 cm)	9 1/2 in. (24.1 cm)	30 in. (76.2 cm)

Skirt (beg along center back, working sideways)

Foundation: Ch 40 (44, 48, 50, 54).

Row 1: Ch 3, dc in 4th ch from hk and ea ch across (40, 44, 48, 50, 54 sts).

Row 2: Ch 3, [ch 1, sk 1, dc in next st] x 20 (22, 24, 25, 27), turn.

Row 3: Ch 3, [ch 1, dc in next ch sp] x 20 (22, 24, 25, 27), turn.

Row 4: Ch 3, dc in ea ch and ch sp across, turn (40, 44, 48, 50, 54 sts).

Rows 5 to 7: Ch 3, dc in ea st across, turn (40, 44, 48, 50, 54 sts).

Repeat rows 2 to seven 9 (10, 11, 12, 12) times.

Repeat rows 2 to 6.

Sew the last row to the foundation row, creating a tube. Weave in end.

23

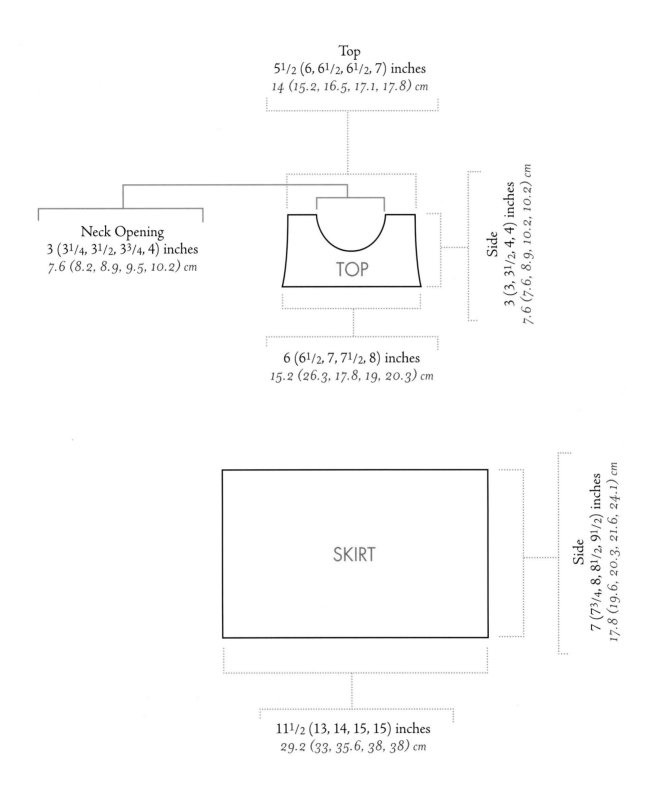

Top
5½ (6, 6½, 6½, 7) inches
14 (15.2, 16.5, 17.1, 17.8) cm

Side
3 (3, 3½, 4, 4) inches
7.6 (7.6, 8.9, 10.2, 10.2) cm

Neck Opening
3 (3¼, 3½, 3¾, 4) inches
7.6 (8.2, 8.9, 9.5, 10.2) cm

TOP

6 (6½, 7, 7½, 8) inches
15.2 (26.3, 17.8, 19, 20.3) cm

SKIRT

Side
7 (7¾, 8, 8½, 9½) inches
17.8 (19.6, 20.3, 21.6, 24.1) cm

11½ (13, 14, 15, 15) inches
29.2 (33, 35.6, 38, 38) cm

Assembly

Mark 1 inch (2.5 cm) (1¹/₂ inches [3.8 cm], 1³/₄ inches [4.4 cm], 2 inches [5.1 cm], 2 inches [5.1 cm]) at ea top side edge of the skirt for the bottom of the armhole opening. Center the seam of the skirt at the center back of the bottom edge of the yoke back. Stitch the remaining top edges of the skirt to the yoke, gathering the skirt beginning about 1 inch (2.5 cm) in from the side edges of the yoke. Sew right front shoulder to right back shoulder.

Finishing

Sc along the armhole and neckline edges, making three sc in the corners of the button hole plackets. Sew buttons to yoke back.

The sample project was made in size 9 to 12 months, using 3¹/₂ skeins (each 125 yards [115m]) of Rowan's Cotton Glace 13/4 ounce (50 g) yarn (100% cotton) in "Glee" #799.

25

SUN HAT

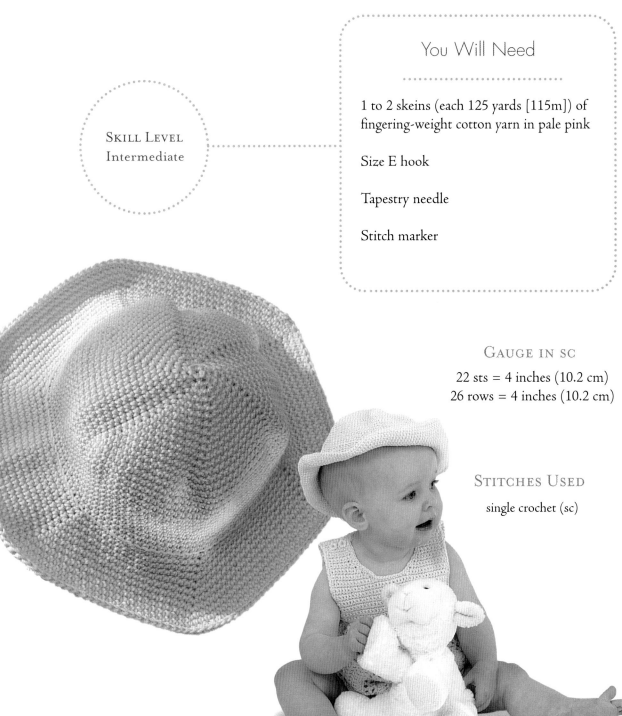

SKILL LEVEL
Intermediate

GAUGE IN SC
22 sts = 4 inches (10.2 cm)
26 rows = 4 inches (10.2 cm)

STITCHES USED
single crochet (sc)

FINISHED MEASUREMENTS

SIZE	HAT CIRCUMFERENCE NOT INCLUDING BRIM
Newborn	14 in. (35.6 cm)
1 to 3 months	16 in. (40.6 cm)
3 to 6 months	17 in. (43.2 cm)
6 to 9 months	18 in. (45.7 cm)
9 to 12 months	19 in. (48.3 cm)

PATTERN NOTES

If it is too difficult to get the hk through the sts in round 2, you can make the sts through the back half of each st for that round, then make the rest through the whole st.

Top of Hat

Round 1: Ch 2, 6 sc in 2nd ch from hk, place marker.

Round 2: 2 sc in ea st around (12 sts).

Round 3: [2 sc in 1st st, sc in next st] 6 times (18 sts).

Round 4: [2 sc in 1st st, sc in next 2 sts] 6 times (24 sts).

Round 5: [2 sc in 1st st, sc in next 3 sts] 6 times, (30 sts).

Continue in patt with 6 increases each round until the hat measures 14 inches (35.6 cm), (16 inches [40.6 cm], 17 inches [43.2 cm], 18 inches [45.7 cm], 19 inches [48.3 cm]) around.

Work even for 10 (11, 12, 13, 13) rounds.

Hat Brim

Count the total number of sts. Divide by six and subtract one from the result. This is A in the instructions following.

Round 1: [sc in back half of next A sts, 2 sc in back half of next st] 6 times.

Round 2: [sc in next (A +1) sts, 2 sc in next st] 6 times.

Round 3 [sc in next (A + 2) sts, 2 sc in next st] 6 times.

Continue in patt with 6 increases ea round until brim measures 1 inch (2.5 cm) (1 inch [2.5 cm], 1$\frac{1}{4}$ inches [3.1 cm], 1$\frac{1}{2}$ inches [3.8 cm], 1$\frac{1}{2}$ inches [3.8 cm]).

Work even for 2 rounds.

Weave in ends.

The sample project was made in size 3 to 6 months, using 1$\frac{1}{2}$ skeins [each 125 yards [115m]) of Rowan's Cotton Glace 1$\frac{3}{4}$ ounce [50g] yarn (100% cotton) in "Glee" #799.

BUTTERCUP FOOTIES

These thick, footed pants are the perfect solution for keeping Baby's tootsies toasty in winter. The classic style is reminiscent of the charming baby clothes of the 1930s, and the buttercup yellow color works for either girls or boys.

You Will Need

2 to 4 skeins (each 131 yards [120 m])
yellow DK-weight yarn

Size G hook

Tapestry needle

Stitch markers

Approximately 1 yard (91.4 cm)
3/4-inch (1.9 cm) wide elastic

Sewing needle and thread to match
yarn color

GAUGE IN SINGLE CROCHET

20 sts = 4 inches (10.2 cm)
24 sts = 4 inches (10.2 cm)

STITCHES USED

single crochet (sc)
double crochet (dc)
2-tr and 3-tr clusters

Finished Measurements

Size	Hip circumference	From top of waistband to heel
Newborn	15 in. (38.1 cm)	9$\frac{1}{2}$ in. (24.1 cm)
1 to 3 months	16$\frac{1}{2}$ in. (41.9 cm)	10 in. (25.4 cm)
3 to 6 months	18$\frac{1}{2}$ in. (47 cm)	11 in. (27.9 cm)
6 to 9 months	19$\frac{1}{2}$ in. (49.5 cm)	12$\frac{1}{2}$ in. (31.8 cm)
9 to 12 months	21 in. (53.34 cm)	13$\frac{1}{2}$ in. (34.3 cm)

Pattern Notes

See the Specialty Stitches section on page 10 for instructions on making the double and triple-crochet clusters for the heels.

Right Toe

Foundation: Ch 4 (4, 5, 5, 6).

Round 1: Ch 1, sc in back half of 2nd ch from hk and back half of next 2 (2, 3, 3, 4) ch, 5 sc in back half of last ch, sc in other half of next 2 (2, 3, 3, 4) ch, 4 sc in last ch, do not turn, place marker (14, 14, 16, 16, 18 sts).

Round 2: Sc in next 4 (4, 5, 5, 6) sts, 2 sc in next 3 sts, sc in next 4 (4, 5, 5, 6) sts, 2 sc in next 3 sts (20, 20, 22, 22, 24 sts).

Rounds 3 to 14: Sc in ea st.

Round 15: Sc in the first 2 sts of the round, turn.

Right Heel

Row 1 to 8: Ch 1, sc in next 15 (15, 16, 16, 17) sts, turn.

Back of Right Heel

Sk next 3 sts, dc in next st, 2-(2, 3, 3, 3) tr cluster in next 2 (2, 3, 3, 3) sts, 3-(3, 2, 2, 3) tr cluster in next 3 (3, 2, 2, 3) sts, 2-(2, 3, 3, 3) tr cluster in next 2 (2, 3, 3, 3) sts, dc in next st, sk 2 sts, sl st in last st, turn.

Right Leg

Round 1: Ch 1, 27 (27, 29, 29, 31) sc around ankle opening, mark side seams.

Rounds 2 to 11: Continue with sc in ea st, inc 2 sts, one at ea marker, on the eighth round.

Round 12 to 19: Beginning on the 12th round increase every other round 5 (7, 9, 11, 12) times (43, 43, 49, 53, 57 sts). Work even for 7 more rounds, ending at the inside side seam, turn. Don't cut the yarn.

Make the left leg the same as the right, but do not turn at the end.

Crotch Gusset

Row 1: On the right leg, continuing from the center inside seam, ch 1, sc in the next 4 (4, 5, 6, 7) sts, turn.

Row 2: Ch 1, sc across, 4 (4, 5, 6, 7) sts.

Cut yarn to a 12-inch (30.5 cm) length; sew the 4 (4, 5, 6, 7) sts to inside edge of left leg. Weave in end.

Body

Using yarn from left leg, make 2 sc across front of gusset, continuing with sc around right leg, then 2 sc across back of gusset, then continuing with sc around left leg (both legs are now joined and you are working in a circle) (74, 82, 92, 98, 104 sts).

Work even for 36 (36, 38, 42, 45) more rows. Weave in end.

Block pants so increases along sides of legs and feet line up evenly.

Waistband

Fold top 7 rows of pants to inside. Using a doubled strand of sewing thread, back stitch through both layers, 2 rows down from the folded edge. Slide the elastic inside the folded edge of crocheting and hold in place. Stitch the last row of crochet to the body, encasing the elastic. When you have stitched all but about 3 inches (7.6 cm), pull the elastic to the baby's waist size, and sew the ends of the elastic tog, clipping off the excess. Finish stitching the seam closed. Weave in ends.

The sample project was made in size 9 to 12 months, using 3½ skeins (each 131 yards [120 m]) of Jaeger Baby Merino DK–weight 1¾–ounce (50g) yarn (100% merino wool) in Buttermilk #205.

PUPPY-FOOTED ONESIE

SKILL LEVEL
Intermediate

The only thing cuter than a puppy is an adorable baby in a puppy-footed onesie. The earflaps are fun for Baby to play with when he discovers his feet, and the puppy zipper pull is a charming detail. This warm onesie is sure to be a bedtime favorite.

You Will Need

3 to 4 skeins (each 131 yards [120 m]) of DK-weight yarn in gray/blue*

1 skein (131 yards [120 m]) of DK-weight yarn in dark blue

Size G hook

Tapestry needle

Stitch markers

16-to 18-inch (40.6 to 45.7 cm) zipper*

Sewing needle and thread to match yarn color

Decorative charm (optional)

Dependent on size of garment

GAUGE IN DOUBLE CROCHET

20 sts = 4 inches (10.2 cm)
10 rows = 4 inches (10.2 cm)

STITCHES USED

single crochet (sc)
double crochet (dc)
2-tr and 3-tr clusters

Pattern Notes

See the Specialty Stitches section on page 10 for instructions on making the double and triple crochet clusters for the heels.

Foot and Leg (make two)

Left Toe

Foundation: Ch 4 (4, 5, 5, 6).

Round 1: Ch 1, sc in back half of 2nd ch from hk and back half of next 2 (2, 3, 3, 4) ch, 5 sc in back half of last ch, sc in other half of next 2 (2, 3, 3, 4) ch, 4 sc in last ch, do not turn, 14 (14, 16, 16, 18) sts.

Round 2: Sc in next 4 (4, 5, 5, 6) sts, 2 sc in next 3 sts, sc in next 4 (4, 5, 5, 6) sts, 2 sc in next 3 sts, 20 (20, 22, 22, 24) sts.

Rounds 3 to 14: Sc in ea st.

Round 15: Sc in the first 2 sts of the round, turn.

Bottom of Left Heel

Rows 1 to 8: Ch 1, sc in next 15 (15, 16, 16, 17) sts, turn.

Back of Left Heel

Sk next 3 sts, dc in next st, 2-(2, 3, 3, 3) tr cluster in next 2 (2, 3, 3, 3) sts, 3-(3, 2, 2, 3) tr cluster in next 3 (3, 2, 2, 3) sts, 2-(2, 3, 3, 3) tr cluster in next 2 (2, 3, 3, 3) sts, dc in next st, sk 2 sts, sl st in last st, turn.

Left Leg

Foundation: Ch 1, 27 (27, 29, 29, 31) sc around ankle opening, join beg to end with a sl st. Continue with sc in ea st for 24 (24, 26, 26, 28) sts. You will be at the center of the inside of the ankle. Mark the outer side "seam," turn. You will now work back and forth.

Row 1: Ch 3, dc in ea st, turn (27, 27, 29, 29, 31 total sts).

Finished Measurements

Size	Width AT CHEST	Length FROM BACK OF NECK TO CROTCH
Newborn	8 in. (20.3 cm)	12 in. (30.5 cm)
1 to 3 months	9 in. (22.9 cm)	13 in. (33 cm)
3 to 6 months	10 in. (25.4 cm)	13$\frac{1}{2}$ in. (34.3 cm)
6 to 9 months	10$\frac{1}{2}$ in. (26.7 cm)	14 in. (35.6 cm)
9 to 12 months	11 in. (27.9 cm)	14$\frac{1}{2}$ in. (36.8 cm)

Rows 2 to 12 (13, 15, 16, 16): Repeat row 1, increasing one stitch on the 2nd and 4th row at the outer side seam marker, by making two dc at marker, 29 (29, 31, 31, 33) total sts. Beginning with the 5th row, increase one at the outer side seam marker and one at the end of each row on every row through row 12 (13, 15, 16, 16), 45 (47, 53, 55, 57) total sts. Cut the yarn to 18 inches (45.7 cm) and sew inner leg seam, weave in end.

Right Foot

Work the same as the left toe, bottom of left heel and back of left heel.

Right Leg

Foundation: Ch 1, 27 (27, 29, 29, 31) sc around ankle opening, join 1st st to last with a sl st. Continue with sc in ea st for 15 sts. You will be at the front corner of the inside of the ankle. Mark the outer side "seam," turn. You will now work back and forth.

Work the same as the left leg, rows 1 to 12 (13, 15, 16, 16), turn.

Crotch: Ch 3, 7 dc. Cut yarn. Weave in end.

Body

Sew the left and right leg together along the 7 dc at the top of the right leg, centering this section over the inner-side seam of the left leg.

Attach a new length of yarn in the first ch of the ch-3 at the beg of the 7 dc. The first row is worked on the wrong side, to keep in patt with the legs.

Row 1: Ch 3, 2 dc along ch 3, 1 dc in ea st on left leg, 3 dc along side of last st of 7 dc (back of crotch), 1 dc in ea st on right leg to the end of the row, 1 dc in turning ch, turn, 82 (86, 98, 102, 106) total sts.

Row 2: Ch 3, dc in ea st across, turn.

Row 3: Ch 3, dc in ea st across, dc in top of ch 3, turn.

Rows 4 to 5: Repeat row 2 and row 3, (84, 88, 100, 104, 108 total sts).

Rows 6 to 22 (24, 24, 25, 25): Work even in dc.

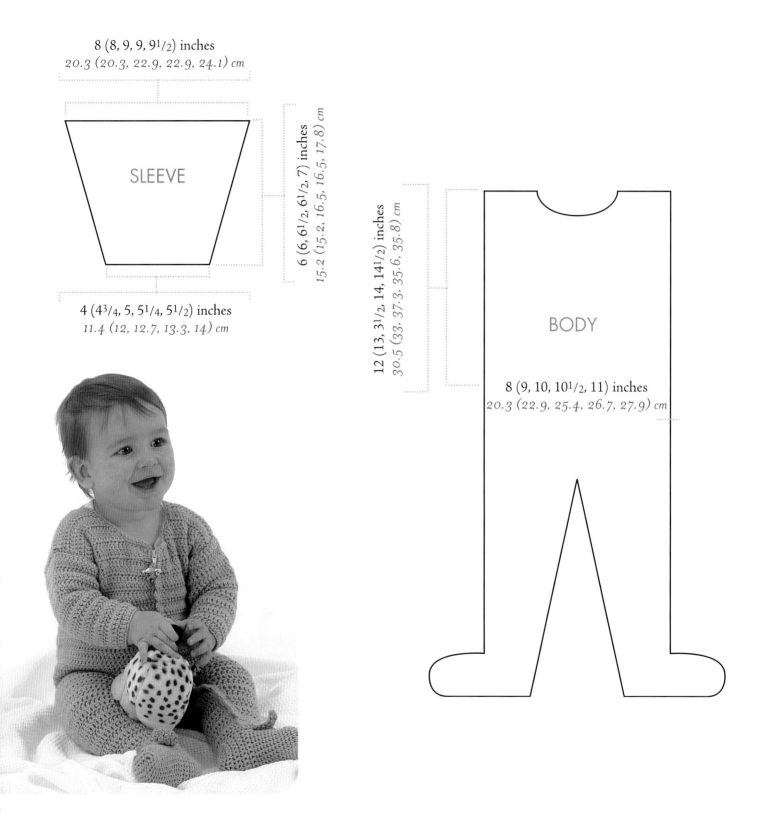

8 (8, 9, 9, 9 1/2) inches
20.3 (20.3, 22.9, 22.9, 24.1) cm

SLEEVE

6 (6, 6 1/2, 6 1/2, 7) inches
15.2 (15.2, 16.5, 16.5, 17.8) cm

4 (4 3/4, 5, 5 1/4, 5 1/2) inches
11.4 (12, 12.7, 13.3, 14) cm

BODY

12 (13, 3 1/2, 14, 14 1/2) inches
30.5 (33, 37.3, 35.6, 35.8) cm

8 (9, 10, 10 1/2, 11) inches
20.3 (22.9, 25.4, 26.7, 27.9) cm

Armhole Opening Front and Back

Rows 23 to 28 (25 to 28, 25 to 29, 26 to 29, 26 to 30): Split sides for front and back. Work ea section separately in dc, 21 (22, 25, 26, 27) sts for ea front section, 42 (44, 50, 52, 54) sts for the back section.

Back

Rows 29 to 34 (29 to 34, 30 to 35, 30 to 35, 31 to 36): Work even in dc.

Weave in end.

Front Neckline

Row 29 (29, 30, 30, 31): Dec 5 (5, 6, 6, 7) sts on ea side of the center front.

On the next 2 rows, dec 1 st at the center front.

Work even for 2 more rows.

Weave in end.

Sleeve (make two)

Foundation: Beg at the wrist, ch 23 (24, 25, 26, 27), turn.

Row 1: Ch 3, dc in 4th ch from hk and ea ch across, turn (23, 24, 25, 26, 27 total sts).

Rows 2 to 17: Ch 3, dc in ea st across, dc in top of ch 3, turn.

Weave in end.

Puppy Ear (make four)

Ch 7, dc in the back half of the 3rd ch from the hk and the next 3 ch, 7 dc in last ch, dc in the other half of the next 4 ch. Cut the tail 12 inches (30.5 cm) long and thread through the last loop. Set aside.

Assembly

Sew front and back shoulder seams tog. Sew sleeve seams. Sew sleeves into armhole openings. Sc around neckline. Position zipper at top of neck opening and sew in place, sewing together excess opening near right ankle beyond the end of the zipper.

Embroidery

Sew two puppy ears to ea foot just before ankle. Using two strands of yarn, make French knots for the eyes and nose on each foot. Make the mouth with small straight stitches. Weave in ends. Sew a decorative button or charm to the zipper pull.

The sample project was made in size 9 to12 months, using 4 skeins (each 131 yards [120m]) of Jaeger Matchmaker Merino DK weight 13/4 ounce (50g) yarn (100% merino wool) in "Nantucket" #879, and 1 skein 135 yards [125m]) of Jaeger Extra-Fine Merino DK weight 13/4 ounce (50g) yarn (100% extra-fine merino wool) in "Ocean" #940.

FINISHED MEASUREMENTS

SIZE	HAT CIRCUMFERENCE
Newborn	14 in. (35.6 cm)
1 to 3 months	16 in. (40.6 cm)
3 to 6 months	17 in. (43.2 cm)
6 to 9 months	18 in. (45.7 cm)
9 to 12 months	19 in. (48.3 cm)

ACORN HAT

This irresistible hat is the perfect topper for an autumn outfit. It looks equally adorable on boys and girls, so it's a great gift if you don't know the gender of the baby you're making it for. Once you know how to make the oak leaves, you can embroider them onto pillows or blankets, too.

GAUGE IN SINGLE CROCHET

24 sts = 4 inches (10.2 cm)
26 rows = 4 inches (10.2 cm)

STITCHES USED

single crochet (sc)
double crochet (dc)
half-double crochet (hdc)

You Will Need

1 skein (131 yards [120m]) DK-weight yarn, light brown

1 skein (131 yards [120m]) of DK-weight in sage green*

Size G hook

Tapestry needle

Stitch marker

You won't need to use the whole skein.

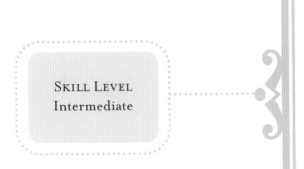

Stem of the Hat

Round 1: Using the brown yarn, ch 2, 5 sc in 2nd ch from hk (5 sts).

Round 2: 1 sc in 1st sc of round 1 and ea sc around (5 sts).

Continue with 1 sc in ea st, spiraling around until stem is about 1¼ inches (3.2 cm) long.

Body of the Hat (continuing from stem)

Round 1: 2 sc in ea st around, place marker (10 sts).

Round 2: [2 sc in 1st st, 1 sc in next st] x 5 (15 sts).

Round 3: [2 sc in 1st st, 1 sc in next 2 sts] x 5 (20 sts).

Continue in patt, increasing 5 st ea round, until hat measures 14 inches (35.6 cm) (16 inches [40.6 cm], 17 inches [43.2 cm], 18 inches [45.7 cm], 19 inches [48.3 cm]).

Work even for 15 (16, 17, 18, 19) rows. Fold hat brim in to wrong side and stitch down to 8th row from end. Weave in end.

Oak Leaf

Half of stem and first "leaf petal": Using the green yarn, ch 12, 1 dc in 3rd ch from hk and next 3 ch.

Remaining leaf petals: [Ch 8, 1 dc in 3rd ch from hk and next 3 ch] x 6.

Finishing Stem

Ch 6. Fold strip in half lengthwise, making sure it doesn't twist. Sl st in 1st ch, next to tail (see figure 1). Make 5 sc through the next 5 ch along both sides of the stem, making ea sc through the back half of the ch closest to you, and the front half of the 1st half of the stem ch, as one.

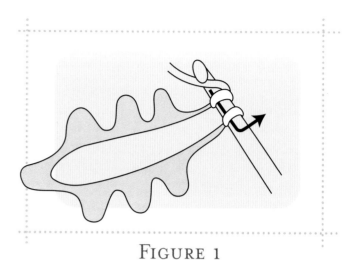

FIGURE 1

Center Section of the Leaf with Center Ridge

Make hdc along the inside edges of the leaf petals, alternating from one side to the other. Making more hdc on one side will make the leaf turn toward the opposite side, making more hdc along both edges will make the leaf longer.

Assembly

Make 2 leaves of differing lengths. Sew the stems of leaves to the top of the hat near the stem. Let the leaves hang loose or arrange them as you chose and tack them down to the hat.

The sample project was made in size 9 to 12 months, using 1 skein (each 131 yards [120 m]) of Jaeger Matchmaker Merino DK-weight 1¾ ounce (50 g) yarn (100% merino wool) in "Soft Camel" # 865 and "Sage" # 857.

HOODED BABY LOUNGER
and Dainty Slippers

This hooded jumper is the perfect outfit for snuggling Baby in comfort after a bath or on a chilly afternoon at home. The tie closure makes it perfect for layering and easy to adapt to an ever-growing baby, so Baby may be able to wear it all winter long. Make the dainty matching slippers for a charming gift set.

SKILL LEVEL
Intermediate

GAUGE IN PATTERN

7 pattern repeats = 4 inches (10.2 cm)
12 rows = 4 inches (10.2 cm)

STITCHES USED

single crochet (sc)
double crochet (dc)

You Will Need

6 to 8 skeins (each 200 yards [183m]) of fingering-weight yarn in green

Size E hook

Tapestry needle

Snap tape*

7/8 yard (80 cm) of 1/2-inch (1.2 cm) wide decorative ribbon

*You can make your own snap tape with decorative ribbon and snaps.

Pattern Notes

Patt rep: [3 dc, ch 2, 1 sc] in Ch–2 sp.

To decrease 1 patt repeat: Work in patt to the last ch sp, 3 dc in ch sp, turn.

To increase 1 patt repeat:

Row 1: [2 dc, ch 1, 1 dc] in 1st st, work in patt across, turn.

Row 2: Work in patt to end of row, [3 dc, ch 1, 1 dc] in ch-1 sp, turn.

Row 3: Ch 3, [2 dc, ch 2, sc] in ch-1 sp, work in patt across, turn (one patt inc complete).

Leg (make two)

Foundation: Ch 47 (47, 50, 53, 53), turn.

Row 1: Ch 3, dc in 4th ch from hk and ea ch across, turn (47, 47, 50, 53, 53 sts).

Row 2: Ch 1 (sk 2, [3 dc, ch 2, 1 sc] in next st) repeat to last 2 sts, 2 dc in last st, turn (15, 15, 16, 17, 17 patt reps).

Row 3: ([3dc, ch 2, 1 sc] in ch-2 sp) repeat across, 2 dc in end of row, turn.

Repeat row 3 until leg measures 8 inches (20.3 cm) 8½ inches [21.6 cm], 9 inches [22.9 cm], 9½ inches [24.1 cm], 10 inches [25.4cm]). Weave in end.

Make another leg the same as the first.

Fold the legs so they open at the inside of the leg.

Begin a new length of yarn at the top left side of the left leg (see figure 1).

Work in patt along the front of the left leg, then the front and back of the right leg, then the back of the left leg. Work 2 patt repeats behind the 1st 2 patt repeats of the row so the side front overlaps the side back, turn.

Work in patt for the next 5 inches (12.7 cm) (5 inches [12.7 cm], 5½ inches [14 cm], 5½ inches [14 cm], 6 inches [15.2 cm], keeping the front left side even and increasing the back left side following the three row inc in the pattern notes section.

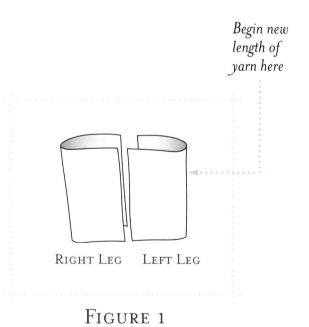

Begin new length of yarn here

RIGHT LEG   LEFT LEG

FIGURE 1

43

FINISHED MEASUREMENTS

SIZE	WIDTH (FINISHED SIZE)	LENGTH (FINISHED SIZE–NOT INCLUDING HOOD)
Newborn	8$1/2$ in. (21.6 cm)	18 in. (45.7 cm)
1 to 3 months	9 in. (22.9 cm)	19 in. (48.3 cm)
3 to 6 months	9$1/2$ in. (24.1 cm)	20 in. (50.8 cm)
6 to 9 months	10 in. (25.4 cm)	21 in. (53.3 cm)
9 to 12 months	10$1/2$ in. (26.7 cm)	22 in. (55.8 cm)

For the next 3 inches (7.6 cm) (3 inches [7.6 cm], 3 inches [7.6 cm], 3$1/2$ inches [8.9 cm], 3$1/2$ inches [8.9 cm]), continue increasing the back left side while beginning to decrease the front left side as in the patt notes.

Separate the front and back sections at the side seams and work separately.

Back: Work even in patt for 4 inches (10.2 cm) (4$1/2$ inches [11.4 cm], 4$1/2$ inches [11.4 cm], 4$1/2$ inches [11.4 cm], 5 inches [12.7 cm]).

Front: Decrease both the right and left fronts until each shoulder width is 3 inches (7.6 cm) (3$1/2$ inches [8.9 cm], 3$1/2$ inches [8.9 cm], 3$1/2$ inches [8.9 cm], 4 inches [10.2 cm]). Work even until the armhole opening measures the same as the back. Weave in end.

Sleeve (make two)

Work the same as for the legs until the sleeve measures 8 inches (20.3 cm) (8$1/2$ inches [21.6 cm], 9 inches [22.9 cm], 9$1/2$ inches [24.1 cm], 10 inches [25.4 cm]) long. Weave in end.

Hood

Foundation: Ch 33 (37, 37, 41, 41), turn.

Row 1: Ch 3, [3 dc, ch 2, 1 sc] in 4th ch from hk, (sk 3 ch, [3 dc, ch 2, 1 sc] in next ch) repeat across, turn (8, 9, 9, 10, 10 total patt repeats). Continue working even in patt until hood measures 14 inches (35.6 cm) (15 inches [38.1 cm], 16 inches [40.6 cm], 17 inches [43.2 cm], 18 inches [45.7 cm]) long. Weave in end.

Assembly

Beg at the sleeve end of the shoulders, sew the front and back shoulders together for 2$1/2$ inches (6.4 cm), (2$1/2$ inches [6.4 cm], 2$1/2$ inches [6.4 cm], 2$1/2$ inches [6.4 cm], 3 inches [7.6 cm]).

Fold hood in half so it is 4$1/2$ inches (11.4 cm) (5 inches [12.7 cm], 5 inches [12.7 cm], 6 inches [15.2 cm], 6 inches [15.2 cm]) by 7 inches (17.8 cm) 7$1/2$ inches [17.8 cm], 8 inches [20.3 cm], 8$1/2$ inches [21.6 cm], 9 inches [22.9 cm]).

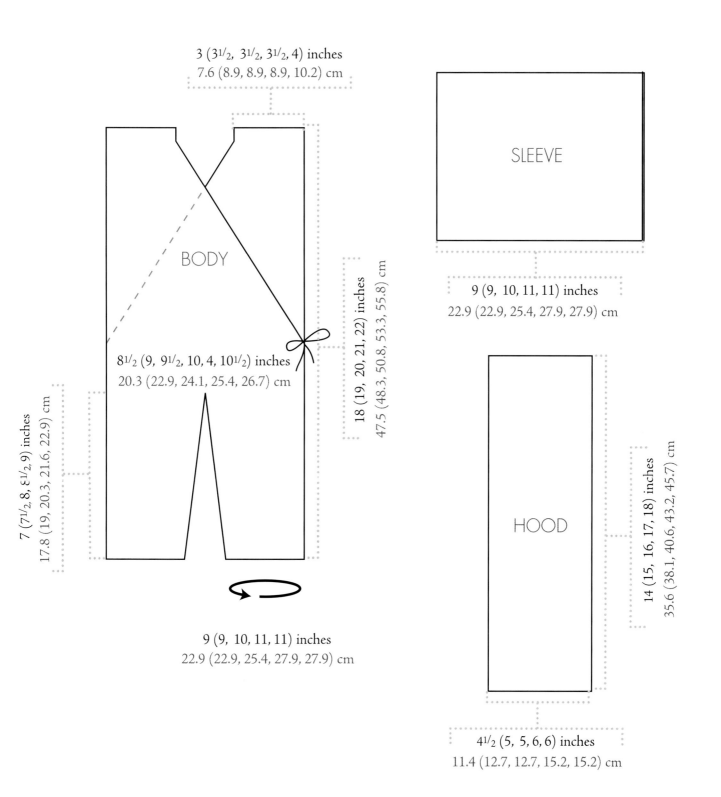

3 (3$^{1}/_{2}$, 3$^{1}/_{2}$, 3$^{1}/_{2}$, 4) inches
7.6 (8.9, 8.9, 8.9, 10.2) cm

SLEEVE

BODY

9 (9, 10, 11, 11) inches
22.9 (22.9, 25.4, 27.9, 27.9) cm

8$^{1}/_{2}$ (9, 9$^{1}/_{2}$, 10, 4, 10$^{1}/_{2}$) inches
20.3 (22.9, 24.1, 25.4, 26.7) cm

18 (19, 20, 21, 22) inches
47.5 (48.3, 50.8, 53.3, 55.8) cm

7 (7$^{1}/_{2}$, 8, 8$^{1}/_{2}$, 9) inches
17.8 (19, 20.3, 21.6, 22.9) cm

HOOD

14 (15, 16, 17, 18) inches
35.6 (38.1, 40.6, 43.2, 45.7) cm

9 (9, 10, 11, 11) inches
22.9 (22.9, 25.4, 27.9, 27.9) cm

4$^{1}/_{2}$ (5, 5, 6, 6) inches
11.4 (12.7, 12.7, 15.2, 15.2) cm

Sew 2 of the long sides tog. This is the center back of the hood. Pin the center back of the hood to the center back of the back neckline and the center front of the hood to the right and left center front neckline of the body (see figure 1). Sew the hood to the neckline. Sew the sleeve seams. Fit the sleeves into the armhole openings and sew in place.

Finishing

Sew 8-inch (20.3 cm) lengths of decorative ribbon to the right and left side openings of the body so you can tie bows to hold the front closed. Turn up the leg bottoms about 1 inch (2.5 cm) and tack in place inside the leg openings. Turn the end of the sleeves up about 1 inch (2.5 cm).

To Make Snap Tape

Pin a length of ribbon to the leg openings extending the ribbon 1/2 -inch (1.2 cm) beyond the bottom of the legs. Remove the ribbon, turn the ends under 1/2 inch (1.2 cm), and sew snaps to the right side of the ribbon at 1 1/2 -inch (3.8 cm) intervals. Repeat on another length of ribbon for the other side of the leg using the companion snap components. Stitch the ribbons in place on the leg openings, gathering the crochet-work slightly at the crotch, if necessary.

The sample project was made in size 9 to 12 months, using 8 skeins (each 200 yards [183m]) of Jaeger Matchmaker Merino 4-Ply 1 3/4 ounce (50g) fin-gering-weight yarn (100% merino wool) in "Croquet" #735.

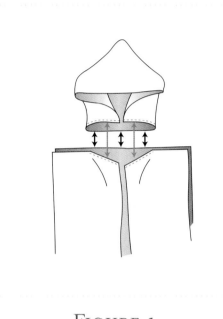

FIGURE 1

46

DAINTY SLIPPERS

You Will Need

1 skein (200 yards [184m]) of fingering-weight yarn in green

Size G hook

Stitch marker

Tapestry needle

1 yard (91.4 cm) of $3/8$-inch (9.5 mm) wide silk ribbon

SKILL LEVEL
Intermediate

GAUGE IN SC
20 sts = 4 inches (10.2 cm)
24 rows = 4 inches (10.2 cm)

STITCHES USED
single crochet (sc)
double crochet (dc)
3-tr and 2-tr cluster

PATTERN NOTES

Use two strands of yarn held together as one throughout.

See the Specialty Stitches section on page 10 for instructions on making the triple-crochet clusters for the heels.

Toe

Foundation: Ch 4 (4, 5, 5, 6).

Round 1: Ch 1, sc in back half of 2nd ch from hk and back half of next 2 (2, 3, 3, 4) ch, 5 sc in back half of last ch, sc in other half of next 2 (2, 3, 3, 4) ch, 4 sc in last ch, do not turn, place marker (14, 14, 16, 16, 18 sts).

Round 2: Sc in next 4 (4, 5, 5, 6) sts, 2 sc in next 3 sts, sc in next 4 (4, 5, 5, 6) sts, 2 sc in next 3 sts (20, 20, 22, 22, 24 sts).

Round 3 to 14: Sc in ea st.

Round 15: Sc in the first 2 sts of the round, turn.

Bottom of Heel

Rows 1 to 8: Ch 1, sc in next 15 (15, 16, 16, 17) sts, turn.

Back of Heel

Sk next 3 sts, dc in next st, 2-(2, 3, 3, 3) tr cluster in next 2 (2, 3, 3, 3) sts, 3-(3, 2, 2, 3) tr cluster in next 3 (3, 2, 2, 3) sts, 2-(2, 3, 3, 3) tr cluster in next 2 (2, 3, 3, 3) sts, dc in next st, sk 2 sts, sl st in last st, turn

Ankle Edging

Row 1: Ch 1, 27 (27, 29, 29, 31) sc around ankle opening, join beg to end with a sl st.

Row 2: Ch 4, [Sk 1, dc, ch 1] repeat around, sl st in 3rd ch of ch-4. Weave in end.

Repeat the instructions to make the 2nd slipper.

Ribbon

Cut the ribbon in half and press. Thread the tapestry needle with one length of ribbon and (beg at the center front of one of the slippers) weave in and out of the dc along row 2 of the ankle edging. Tie the ribbon into a bow and cut the ribbon tails to about 2 inches (5.1 cm) long. Repeat for the other ribbon and bootie.

The sample project was made in size 9 to 12 months, using 1 skein (200 yards [183m]) of Jaeger Matchmaker Merino 4-ply fingering-weight 1¾ 1ounce (50g) yarn (100% merino wool) in "Croquet" #735.

FINISHED MEASUREMENTS

SIZE	TOE TO HEEL (FINISHED SIZE)
Newborn	3½ in. (8.8 cm)
1 to 3 months	3¾ in. (9.5 cm)
3 to 6 months	4 in. (10.2 cm)
6 to 9 months	4¼ in. (10.7 cm)
9 to 12 months	4½ in. (11.43 cm)

RASCAL HAT

This playful boy's hat has a delightful nostalgic look. The wedge-shaped construction might look intimidating, but don't worry. Working each color section lengthwise, one at a time, makes the color work easy. Pair it with the ball on page 54 for a perfect gift.

GAUGE IN SINGLE CROCHET

20 sts = 4 inches (10.2 cm)
11 rows = 4 inches (10.2 cm)

STITCHES USED

single crochet (sc)
double crochet (dc)
half-double crochet (hdc)

You Will Need

1 skein (131 yards [120m]) each of
DK-weight yarn in blue, green and yellow

Size E hook

Tapestry needle

Stitch marker

Hat

Foundation: Using the blue yarn, ch 14 (18, 21, 25), turn.

Row 1: Ch 1 beginning in 2nd ch from hk, and working one st in ea ch across, 5 (6, 7, 8) sc, 4 (5, 6, 7) hdc, 5 (7, 8, 10) dc, turn.

Row 2: Ch 3, 5 (7, 8, 10) dc, 4 (5, 6, 7) hdc, 1 (1, 2, 3) sc, 1 sl st, turn.

Row 3: Ch 1, sk 1, 1 sl st, 1 (1, 2, 2) sc, 4 (5, 6, 7) hdc, 4 (7, 8, 10) dc, turn.

Row 4: Ch 3, 5 (7, 8, 10) dc, 4 (5, 6, 7) hdc, 4 (5, 6, 7) sc, 1 sl st pulling the green yarn through the last half of the st.

Repeat rows 1 to 4 8 (9, 10, 11) more times, repeating the blue, green, yellow color sequence (on size 1 to 3 months, change the last color to green rather than blue). After the last repeat, cut the yarn 18 inches (46 cm) long. Pass through the last lp and st the last row to the 1st row. Weave in end.

Bottom Band

Attach the blue yarn to the inside bottom edge of the hat between a blue and green section, so that you will be working first over the green section. Working from the inside of the hat, make 9 sc for ea color section along the bottom of the hat, joining the first st to the last with a sl st, mark beg (81, 90, 99, 108 total sts).

Ch 1, sc in ea st around, joining beg to end with sl st. Repeat for a total of 5 rows, including the first row. Keep yarn attached for the first triangle.

Triangles

For the first triangle, continue using the blue yarn from the bottom band of the hat, work rows 1 to 8 below.

Row 1: Ch 1, 9 sc, turn.

Row 2: Ch 1, sk 1st st, 8 sc, turn.

Row 3: Ch 1, sk 1st st, 7 sc, turn.

Row 4: Ch 1, sk 1st st, 6 sc, turn.

Row 5: Ch 1, sk 1st st, 5 sc, turn.

Row 6: Ch 1, sk 1st st, 4 sc, turn.

Row 7: Ch 1, sk 1st st, 3 sc, turn.

Row 8: Ch 1, sk 1st, st 2-sc cluster, cut yarn, weave in end.

Attach the next color of yarn to the left of the triangle you just made and follow rows 1 to 8 above. Repeat for each triangle around the hat, in the same color sequence as the hat. Weave in all ends.

Button

Using the blue yarn, ch 4, 15 dc in 4th ch from hk. Join with a sl st to form a circle. Stitch over the opening at the top of the hat.

FINISHED MEASUREMENTS

SIZE	HAT CIRCUMFERENCE
Newborn	14 in. (35.5 cm)
1 to 3 months	16 in. (40.64 cm)
3 to 9 months	17 $1/2$ in. (44.45 cm)
9 to 12 months	19 in. (48.26 cm)

The sample project was made in size 9 to 12 months, using 1 skein (131 yards [120m]) each of Jaeger Matchmaker Merino DK-weight 1¾ ounce (50g) yarn (100% merino wool) in "Pacific" #889, "Asparagus #886, and "Butter" #862.

BABY'S FIRST BALL

SKILL LEVEL
Easy

A soft crochet ball is a perfect first toy for Baby. There's no need to worry about sharp edges or choking hazards. Baby can roll the ball, put it in his mouth, or scrunch it up with his hands. Balls are quick, easy, and fun to make in any size with just about any yarn. Variegated yarn adds interest to the ball.

You Will Need

1 skein (131 yards [120 m]) of worsted-weight variegated yarn

Size G hook

Tapestry needle

Polyester fiberfill

Stitch marker

STITCHES USED

single crochet (sc)

53

PATTERN NOTES

Make your stitches tight so the stuffing doesn't show through the stitches.

FINISHED MEASUREMENTS

Small: Approximately 3-inch (7.6 cm) diameter
Large: Approximately 6-inch (15.2 cm) diameter

Small Ball

Foundation and Round 1: Ch 2, 6 sc in 2nd ch from hk, place marker.

Round 2: 2 sc in ea st around (12 sts).

Round 2: [1 sc, 2 sc in next st] repeat around (18 sts).

Round 3: [2 sc, 2 sc in next st] repeat around (24 sts).

Round 4: [3 sc, 2 sc in next st] repeat around (30 sts).

Round 5: [4 sc, 2 sc in next st] repeat around (36 sts).

Continue in pattern, increasing 6 sts ea round until the colors in the variegated yarn begin to line up with the previous round. Work even until the ball is about three-quarters the size of a round ball shape. Make 6 evenly spaced decreases along the next round. Continue decreasing in the same 6 stitches ea round until the ball opening is about 1 1/2-inch (3.8 cm) in diameter. Stuff the ball and continue decreasing until you have 6 sts in the round, then cut the yarn to about 12 inches (30.5 cm) and close the hole by stitching across several of the last stitches in the last round with a tapestry needle and weave in the end.

Larger Ball

To make the larger ball, begin the same as for the small ball through round 5, then continue increasing in pattern. The colors will line up once, but continue increasing until they go out of alignment, then begin to line up again when the shape is larger. Work even until the ball is about three-quarters the size of a round ball shape and finish the same as for the small ball.

The sample projects were made using 1 skein of Bernat Handicrafter Cotton, worsted-weight 1 1/2 ounce (42.5g) yarn (100% cotton) in Sage/Lavender #48 for the large ball, and Country Sage Ombre #23233 for the small ball.

ORANGE SLICE BALL

This ball can be paired with the Rascal Hat on page 49 for a memorable gift.

Hat on page 49 for a memorable gift.

SKILL LEVEL
Intermediate

You Will Need

1 skein (131 yards [120m]) of DK-weight yarn in each of the following colors: blue, green, and yellow

Size E hook

Tapestry needle

Polyester fiberfill

FINISHED MEASUREMENTS
5-inch (12.7 cm) diameter

GAUGE IN SINGLE CROCHET
20 sts = 4 inches (10.2 cm)
11 rows = 4 inches (10.2 cm)

STITCHES USED
single crochet (sc)
double crochet (dc)
half-double crochet (hdc)

Pass through the last lp and st the last row to the first row, stuffing the ball when you've stitched half way across the opening, then finish stitching the ball closed.

The sample project was made using 1 skein (131 yards [120m]) each of Jaeger Matchmaker Merino DK-weight 1¾ ounce [50g] yarn (100% merino wool) in "Pacific" #889, "Asparagus #886, and "Butter" #862.

PATTERN NOTES

Make the stitches tight so the stuffing doesn't show through the stiches.

Ball

Foundation: Using the blue yarn, ch 25, turn.

Row 1: Ch 1, 5 sc, 5 hdc, 5 dc, 5 hdc, 2 sc, 1 sl st, turn.

Row 2: Ch 1, sk 1st st, 1 sl st, 1 sc, 5 hdc, 5 dc, 5 hdc, 2 sc, 1 sl st, turn.

Row 3: Ch 1, sk 1st st, 1 sl st, 1 sc, 5 hdc, 5dc, 5 hdc, 2 sc, 1 sc in row 1, 1 sl st in foundation, turn.

Row 4: Ch 1, 1 sl st, 4 sc, 5 hdc, 5 dc, 5 hdc, 1 sc, 3 sc in row 1, 1 sl st, pulling a new color of yarn through the last half of the stitch.

Repeat rows 1 to 4 eight more times, following the color sequence of the sample, or your own arrangement. Cut the yarn 18 inches (45.7 cm) long.

COOL COTTON SUNDRESS

On a hot summer's day, this cool cotton sundress will keep Baby comfortable and stylish. The under-layer is constructed like a onesie, which is hidden by the apron on top. The simple straps tie in bows, letting you adjust the size to fit the baby.

GAUGE IN SINGLE CROCHET

21 sts = 4 inches
24 rows = 4 inches

STITCHES USED

single crochet (sc)
double crochet (dc)

You Will Need

1 skein (184 yards [170m]) of fingering-weight cotton yarn in pale pink

1 skein (184 yards [170m]) of fingering-weight cotton yarn in pink

Size E hook

Tapestry needle

Small snap closures

1/4 yard (22 cm) decorative ribbon

Sewing needle and thread to match ribbon

57

Finished Measurements

Size	Width	Length
Newborn	6 in. (15.2 cm)	8$\frac{1}{2}$ in. (21.6 cm)
1 to 3 months	6 in. (15.2 cm)	9 in. (22.9 cm)
3 to 6 months	7 in. (17.8 cm)	9$\frac{1}{2}$ in. (24.1 cm)
6 to 9 months	7 in. (17.8 cm)	9$\frac{1}{2}$ in. (24.1 cm)
9 to 12 months	7 in. (17.8 cm)	10 in. (25.4 cm)

Pattern Notes

The bottom part of the under-layer is made up of open shells (2dc, ch 1, 2 dc) and the top half is made with an openwork chain netting. The ch 4 at the beg of the rows count as a dc in the first shell of the row.

Back of Under-Layer (beg at crotch closing)

Foundation: Using the pale pink yarn, ch 10 (10, 13, 13, 13).

Row 1: Ch 1, sc in 2nd ch from hk and ea ch across, turn.

Rows 2 to 6: Ch 1, sc in ea st across, turn.

Row 7: Ch 4, [dc, ch 1, 2 dc] in 1st st, (sk 2, [2 dc, ch 1, 2 dc] in next st) 2 (2, 3, 3, 3) times, [2 dc, ch 1, 2 dc] in last st, turn (4, 4, 5, 5, 5 total shells).

Row 8: Ch 4, dc in 1st st, ([2 dc, ch 1, 2 dc] in next ch sp) repeat across, 2 dc in last st, turn.

Row 9: Ch 4 [dc, ch 1, 2 dc] in 1st st, ([2dc, ch 1, 2 dc] in next ch sp) repeat across, making the last shell between the ch 4 and 1 dc at the end of the row, turn (6, 6, 7, 7, 7 total shells).

Rows 10 to 13: Repeat row 8 and row 9 (10, 10, 11, 11, 11 total shells).

Rows 14 and 15: Ch 4, [dc, ch 1, 2 dc] in 4 th ch from hk, work in patt across (12, 12, 13, 13, 13 total shells).

Rows 15 to 20: Work even in patt.

(Begin openwork section of top half of under-layer here.)

Row 21: [Ch 5, sc in ch sp], repeat across, dc in end of last shell, turn.

Rows 22 to 25 (to 26, 27, 28, 29): [Ch 5, sc in ch sp] repeat across 22, turn.

Row 26 (27, 28, 29, 30): [Ch 3, sc in ch sp] repeat across, turn.

Row 27 (28, 29, 30, 31): Ch 3, dc in ea st.

Weave in end.

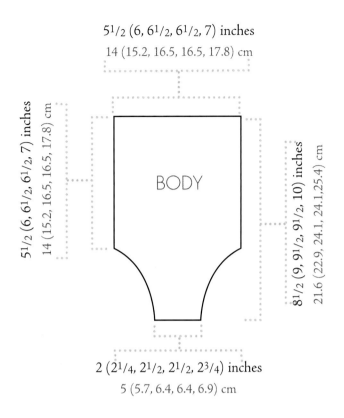

5½ (6, 6½, 6½, 7) inches
14 (15.2, 16.5, 16.5, 17.8) cm

5½ (6, 6½, 6½, 7) inches
14 (15.2, 16.5, 16.5, 17.8) cm

BODY

8½ (9, 9½, 9½, 10) inches
21.6 (22.9, 24.1, 24.1,25.4) cm

2 (2¼, 2½, 2½, 2¾) inches
5 (5.7, 6.4, 6.4, 6.9) cm

APRON

6 (6½, 7, 7, 7½) inches
15.2 (16.5, 17.8, 17.8, 19) cm

Front of Under-Layer
(beg at crotch closing)

Foundation: Using the pale pink yarn, ch 10 (10, 13, 13, 13), turn.

Row 1: Ch 1, sc in 2nd ch from hk and ea ch across, turn.

Rows 2 to 6: Ch 1, sc in ea st across, turn.

Row 7: Ch 4, [dc, ch 1, 2 dc] in 2nd st, (sk 2, [2 dc, ch 1, 2 dc] in next st) 2 (2, 3, 3, 3) times, turn, 3 (3, 4, 4, 4) total shells.

Row 8: Ch 4, dc in 1st st, ([2 dc, ch 1, 2 dc] in next ch sp) repeat across, 2 dc in last st, turn.

Row 9 : Ch 4, [dc, ch 1, 2 dc] in 1st st, ([2 dc, ch 1, 2 dc] in next ch sp) repeat across, making the last shell between the ch 4 and 1 dc at the end of the row, turn (5, 5, 6, 6, 6 total shells).

Row 10: Ch 4, [dc, ch 1, 2 dc] in the 1st ch sp, [2dc, ch 1, 2 dc] in ea ch sp across, turn.

Row 11 and 12: Repeat row 8 and row 9, for (7, 7, 8, 8, 8 total shells).

Row 13 and 14: Ch 6, [dc, ch 1, 2 dc] in 4th ch from hk, sk 2 [2 dc ch 1, 2 dc] in next ch, work in patt across (11, 11, 12, 12, 12 total shells).

Rows 15 to 20: Work even in patt.

(Begin openwork section for top half of under-layer.)

Rows 21 to 25 (26, 27, 28, 29): [Ch 5, sc in ch sp] repeat across, dc in end of last shell, turn.

Row 26 (27, 28, 29, 30): [Ch 3, sc in ch sp] repeat across, turn.

Row 27 (28, 29, 30, 31): Ch 3, dc in ea st.

Weave in end.

Apron (working from side to side)

Foundation: Using the pink yarn, ch 33 (35, 37, 41, 45), turn.

Row 1: Ch 4, dc in the 5th ch from hk, [sk 1, ch 1, dc in next ch] repeat across, turn.

Row 2: Ch 4, dc in ch sp, [ch 1, dc in next ch sp] repeat across, turn.

Rows 3 to 39 (39, 41, 41, 41): Repeat row 2.

Weave in end.

Strap (make four)

Foundation: Ch 42 (44, 46, 48, 50), making the slip knot about 12 inches (30.5 cm) from the end, turn.

Row 1: Ch 1, sc in 2nd ch from hk and ea ch across.

Cut yarn to 12 inches (30.5 cm), pull through last st, set aside.

Assembly and Finishing

Sew side seams of front and back under-layer. Cut ribbon to 1/2 inch (1.3 cm) longer than the width of the crotch. Turn ends of ribbon under 1/4 inch (6 mm) and baste ends in place. Sew snaps to ribbon and sew ribbon to crotch of under-layer. Sew straps to the top of the under-layer, about 11/2 inches (3.8 cm) from the center front and center back. Tie the straps into bows. Attach the pink yarn to a corner of the apron, ch 2, then sc in the back of the under-layer just below the row of dc and one st from the strap toward the armhole. *Ch 3, sc in the next row of the apron, ch 3, sc in the next st on the under-layer* repeat between asterisks around to the other side of the back of the under-layer. Weave in ends.

The sample project was made in size 9 to 12 months, using 1 skein (184 yards [170m]) each of Rowan 4-Ply fingering-weight 13/4 ounce (50g) cotton yarn (100% cotton) in "Orchid" #120 and "Allure" #119.

PLAYFUL OVERALLS

A cute and comfortable pair of overalls is a must for every baby. These are soft and flexible so they're easy to get into and out of, and the snap closures in the legs give easy access for changing. Make these overalls in cotton yarn for spring or wool for fall or winter.

SKILL LEVEL
Intermediate

STITCHES USED

single crochet (sc)
double crochet (dc)
half-double crochet (hdc)
front-post double crochet (fpdc)
back-post double crochet (bpdc)

GAUGE IN DOUBLE CROCHET
(holding two strands together
as one, using the H hook)

15 sts = 4 inches (10.2 cm)
8 rows = 4 inches (10.2 cm)

You Will Need

3 to 4 skeins (each 200 yards [183 m]) green fingering-weight yarn

1 skein (131 yards [120m]) yellow fingering weight yarn

Size E hook

Size H hook

Tapestry needle

Set of 1-inch (2.5 cm) long overalls closure or two $3/8$-inch (9.5 mm) buttons

Snap tape, or bias tape and snaps

Right Leg

Use 2 strands of green yarn held together as one, and the H hk.

Foundation: Ch 24 (26, 30, 30, 34), turn.

Row 1: Ch 3, dc in 4th ch from hk and ea ch across, turn (24, 26, 28, 28, 30 total sts).

Rows 2 to 7 (to 8, 9,10, 10): Ch 3, dc in ea st across, dc in top of ch 3, turn (one inc at end of ea row) (30, 33, 38, 39, 43 total sts).

Work even for the next 3 (3, 4, 4, 5) rows.

At the end of the last row, ch 3 (3, 4, 4, 5), cut the yarn to 12 inches (30.5 cm), pass through the last st, set aside.

Left Leg and Body

Use 2 strands of green yarn and the H hk.

Work the same as the right leg, except at the end of the last row, ch 3 (3, 4, 4, 5), then join to the right leg with a sl st in the top corner of the right leg piece. Attach the end of the right leg yarn to the other top corner of the left leg so the two legs are joined in a circle along the top row. Pick up the left leg yarn, turn, ch 4, dc in ea st and ch around the legs to the end of the row, turn. Work even for 10 (12, 14, 14, 16) more rows. Cut the yarn to 18 inches (45.7 cm), pass through the last st, and sew the body tog at the back seam. Weave in end.

Chest Piece

Use one strand of green yarn and E hk, and beg at the top edge and working down.

Foundation: Ch 35 (39, 41, 43, 43), turn.

Row 1: Ch 3, dc in 4th ch from hk and ea ch across (35, 39, 41, 43, 43 total sts).

Row 2: Ch 3, sk 1st st, [2 fpdc, 2 bpdc] repeat to the last two sts, 2 fpdc, hdc in top of ch 3, turn.

Repeat [row 2] 1(1, 2, 3, 4) time.

Five row increase (increase two sts at ea side in patt [2 fpdc, 2 bpdc]):

Increase Row 1: Ch 3, hdc in 1st st, work in patt across, 2 dc in top of ch 3, turn.

Increase Row 2 to 3: Ch 3, bpdc in 2nd st, work in patt across, 1 bpdc in last st, hdc in top of ch 3, turn.

Increase Row 4: Ch 3, hdc in 1st st, bpdc, work in patt across ending with a bpdc in the last st, 2 dc in top of ch 3, turn.

Increase Row 5: Ch 3, sk 1 st, work in patt across, hdc in top of ch 3, turn.

Repeat 5-row increase rows 2 more times.

Work even for 0 (2, 2, 2, 3) rows.

Cut the yarn to 24 inches (61 cm), pass through last st. Set aside.

Pocket

Use one strand of yellow yarn and E hk.

Foundation: Ch 1, turn.

Row 1: Ch 1, 3 sc in 2nd ch from hk, turn.

Row 2: Ch 1, 2 sc in ea st, turn, 6 total sts.

Row 3: Ch 1, [1 sc, 2 sc in next st] three times, turn (9 total sts).

Row 4: Ch 1, [2 sc, 2 sc in next st] three times, turn (12 total sts).

Row 5: Ch 1, [3 sc, 2 sc in next st] three times, turn (15 total sts).

Row 6: Ch 1, [4 sc, 2 sc in next st] three times, turn (18 total sts).

Row 7: Ch 1, [5 sc, 2 sc in next st] three times, do not turn (21 total sts).

Row 8: Ch 1, 14 sc across the top of the pocket, turn.

Row 9 to 12: Ch 1, sc in ea st, turn.

Cut yarn to 18 inches (45.7 cm), pass through the last st, set pocket aside.

Strap (make two)

(Use one strand of green yarn and the E hk)

Foundation: Ch 6, turn.

Row 1: Ch 1, sc in 2nd ch from hk and ea ch across, turn.

Row 2: Ch 1, sc in ea st across, turn.

Repeat row 2 until the strap measures 8¹/₂ inches (21.6 cm) (9 inches [22.9 cm], 9¹/₂ inches [24.1 cm], 10 inches [25.4 cm], 10¹/₂ inches [26.7 cm]) long. Cut yarn to 12 inches (30.5 cm) pass through last st, set aside.

Finishing

Sc along the sides of the inside leg edges, making 8 dc at the top of the legs. Sew snap tape along the edges of the leg seams, or make your own snap tape by attaching snaps to bias tape and sew that to the leg seams. Sew the chest piece to the top edge of the body. Sew the pocket to the chest piece using the 18-inch (45.7 cm) tail of yellow yarn. Sew ea strap to the top of the body, about 1 1/2 inches (3.8 cm) to 2 inches (5.1 cm) from the center back seam and angled in towards the center back. Cross the straps over ea other about 3 inches (7.6 cm) from the body and sew together. Thread the other ends of the straps through the overall closures and sew in place. If you use buttons instead of closures, sew them to the chest piece about 1 inch (2.5 cm) in from the top corners.

The sample project was made in size 6 to 9 months, using 4 skeins (each 200 yards [183 m]) of Jaeger Matchmaker Merino 4-ply 1 3/4 ounces (50g) fingering-weight yarn, (100% merino wool) in "Thyme" #715 and 1 skein (200 yards [183m]) of Jaeger Baby Merino 4-ply weight 1 3/4 ounce (50g) yarn (100% merino wool) in "Buttermilk" #105.

FINISHED MEASUREMENTS

SIZE	WIDTH	LENGTH
Newborn	8 in. (20.3 cm)	14$\frac{1}{2}$ in. (36.8 cm)
1 to 3 months	9 in. (22.9 cm)	16$\frac{1}{2}$ in. (41.9 cm)
3 to 6 months	10 in. (25.4 cm)	18$\frac{1}{2}$ in. (47 cm)
6 to 9 months	10$\frac{1}{2}$ in. (26.7 cm)	19$\frac{1}{2}$ in. (49.5 cm)
9 to 12 months	11$\frac{1}{2}$ in. (29.2 cm)	21 in. (53.34 cm)

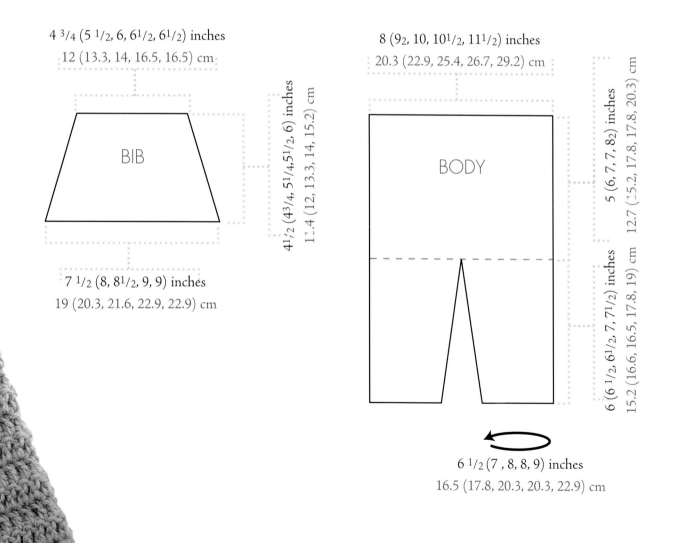

4 3/4 (5 1/2, 6, 6^1/2, 6^1/2) inches

12 (13.3, 14, 16.5, 16.5) cm

BIB

4^1/2 (4^3/4, 5^1/4, 5^1/2, 6) inches

11.4 (12, 13.3, 14, 15.2) cm

7 1/2 (8, 8^1/2, 9, 9) inches

19 (20.3, 21.6, 22.9, 22.9) cm

8 (9$_2$, 10, 10^1/2, 11^1/2) inches

20.3 (22.9, 25.4, 26.7, 29.2) cm

BODY

5 (6, 7, 7, 8$_2$) inches

12.7 (15.2, 17.8, 17.8, 20.3) cm

6 (6 ^{1}/2, 6^1/2, 7, 7^1/2) inches

15.2 (16.6, 16.5, 17.8, 19) cm

6 1/2 (7 , 8, 8, 9) inches

16.5 (17.8, 20.3, 20.3, 22.9) cm

67

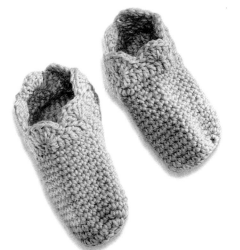

DUSTY ROSE SWEATER
and Matching Booties

SKILL LEVEL
Intermediate

The secret to this impossibly soft sweater is luxurious alpaca wool. Sweet details like raglan sleeves and mother-of-pearl buttons add charm to this classic pattern. Make the soft booties on page 72 to match for a truly special outfit.

Stitches Used

single crochet (sc)
double crochet (dc)

Gauge in pattern repeat

14 sts = 4 inches (10.2 cm)
12 rows = 4 inches (10.2 cm)

You Will Need

3 to 5 skeins (200 yards [184m]) of finger-ing-weight rose-colored alpaca yarn*

Size G hook

Size H hook

Tapestry needle

5 or 6 mother-of-pearl buttons, each about
$1/2$-inch (1.3 cm) in diameter *

Sewing needle and thread in a color to
match buttons or yarn

Amount depends on the size of the garment

FINISHED MEASUREMENTS

SIZE	WIDTH	LENGTH
Newborn	10 in. (25.4 cm)	8 in. (20.3 cm)
1 to 3 months	10½ in. (26.7 cm)	8½ in. (21.6 cm)
3 to 6 months	11 in. (27.9 cm)	9 in. (22.9 cm)
6 to 9 months	11½ in. (29.2 cm)	9½ in. (24.1 cm)
9 to 12 months	12 in. (20.5 cm)	10 in. (26.7 cm)

PATTERN NOTES

Use two strands of yarn held together as one throughout and the size H hook for the body and sleeves.

Use a single strand of yarn and the size G hook for the single crochet plackets and neckband.

Back

Foundation: Ch 36 (38, 40, 42, 44), turn.

Row 1: Ch 3, sc in 4th ch from hk, [dc, sc] repeat to the last ch, dc in the last ch, turn.

Row 2: Ch 1, [sc, dc] repeat across, turn.

Rows 3 to 15 (16, 18, 20, 22): Ch 1, [sc in dc, dc in sc] across, ending with a dc in the last st, turn.

Back Armhole Shaping

Row 1: Ch 1, sc in 1st 2 (2, 3, 3, 4) sts, work in patt to last 2 (2, 3, 3, 4) sts, turn.

Row 2: Ch 1, sk 1st st, work in patt to last 2 (2, 3, 3, 4) sts, turn.

Row 3: Ch 1, sk 1st st, work in patt across ending with dc, turn.

Rows 4 to 10: Repeat row 3. Weave in ends.

70

Right Front

Foundation: Ch 16 (16, 18, 18, 20), turn.

Work as for back to armhole shaping.

Right Front Armhole Shaping

Row 1: Ch 1, sc in next 2 (2, 3, 3, 4) sts, work in patt across, turn, 14 (14, 15, 15, 16) total sts.

Row 2: Work in patt, turn.

Row 3: Ch 1, sk 2 sts, work in patt across, turn, 12 (12, 13, 13, 14) total sts.

Row 4: Work in patt, turn.

Row 5: Repeat row 3, 10 (10, 11, 11, 12) total sts.

Row 6: Work in patt, turn.

Row 7: Repeat row 3, 8 (8, 8, 8, 10) total sts.

Row 8: Work in patt, turn.

Row 9: Ch 1, sk 2 sts, work in patt for next 4 (4, 4, 4, 6) sts, turn.

For largest size only: Ch 1, sk next 2 sts, work in patt for next 4 sts, turn.

Row 10 (10, 10, 10, 11): Ch 1, sk 2 sts, work in patt for 2 sts.

Weave in end.

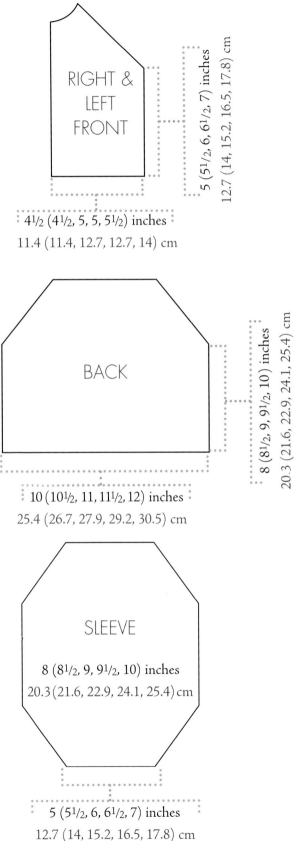

RIGHT & LEFT FRONT

5 (5½, 6, 6½, 7) inches
12.7 (14, 15.2, 16.5, 17.8) cm

4½ (4½, 5, 5, 5½) inches
11.4 (11.4, 12.7, 12.7, 14) cm

BACK

8 (8½, 9, 9½, 10) inches
20.3 (21.6, 22.9, 24.1, 25.4) cm

10 (10½, 11, 11½, 12) inches
25.4 (26.7, 27.9, 29.2, 30.5) cm

SLEEVE

8 (8½, 9, 9½, 10) inches
20.3 (21.6, 22.9, 24.1, 25.4) cm

5 (5½, 6, 6½, 7) inches
12.7 (14, 15.2, 16.5, 17.8) cm

Left Front

Work the same as for back to one row less than right front (this causes the armhole shaping to be on the opposite side of the finished piece).

Work as for right front armhole shaping.

Weave in end.

Sleeve (make two)

Foundation: Ch 18 (20, 22, 24, 26), turn.

Row 1: Ch 3, sc in 4th ch from hk, [dc, sc] repeat to the lst ch, dc in last ch, turn.

Row 2: Ch 1, [sc in dc, dc in sc] repeat across, ending with a dc in sc, turn.

Work even in patt for 1 (3, 5, 7, 8) rows more, turn.

Increase Rows

Rows 1 to 2: Ch 3, dc in 3rd ch from hk, work in patt across, turn 19 (21, 23, 25, 27 total sts).

Rows 3 to 4: Work even in patt, turn.

Repeat increase rows 3 more times (27, 29, 31, 33, 35 total sts).

Work even for 2 (2, 3, 3, 4) rows.

Decrease Rows

Row 1: Ch 1, sk 2 sts, work in patt across, turn, 2 sts decreased.

Repeat decrease row 9 more times.

Weave in end.

Assembly

Sew front of sleeves to front armholes, sew back of sleeves to back armholes. Sew sleeve seams and side seams.

Right Front Placket

Foundation: Using the size G hk, make 44 sc along the side of the center front.

Rows 1 to 2: Ch 1, sc in ea st across, turn.

Row 3: Ch 1, [6 sc, ch 2, sk 2] repeat 5 times, 4 sc, turn.

Rows 4 to 5: Repeat row 1.

Weave in end.

Left Front Placket

Foundation: Using the size G hk, make 34 (36, 40, 42, 44) sc along the side of the center front.

Rows 1 to 5: Ch 1, sc in ea st across, turn.

Weave in end.

Neckband

Using size G hk, make 14 (15, 15, 16, 16) sc along the right front placket and right front, 8 (8, 9, 9, 10) sc along the right sleeve, 20 (20, 21, 21, 22) sc along the back, 8 (8, 9, 9, 10) along the left sleeve and 14 (15, 15, 16, 16) sc along the left front placket and left front (76 sts).

Rows 1 to 4: Ch 1, sc in ea st across, turn.

Weave in end.

Finishing

Sew buttons to left placket across from button-holes.

The sample project was made in size 9 to 12 months, using 5 skeins (each 200 yards [184m]) of Jaeger Alpaca 4-ply weight 1 3/4 ounce (50g) yarn (100% alpaca) in "Down" #384.

MATCHING BOOTIES

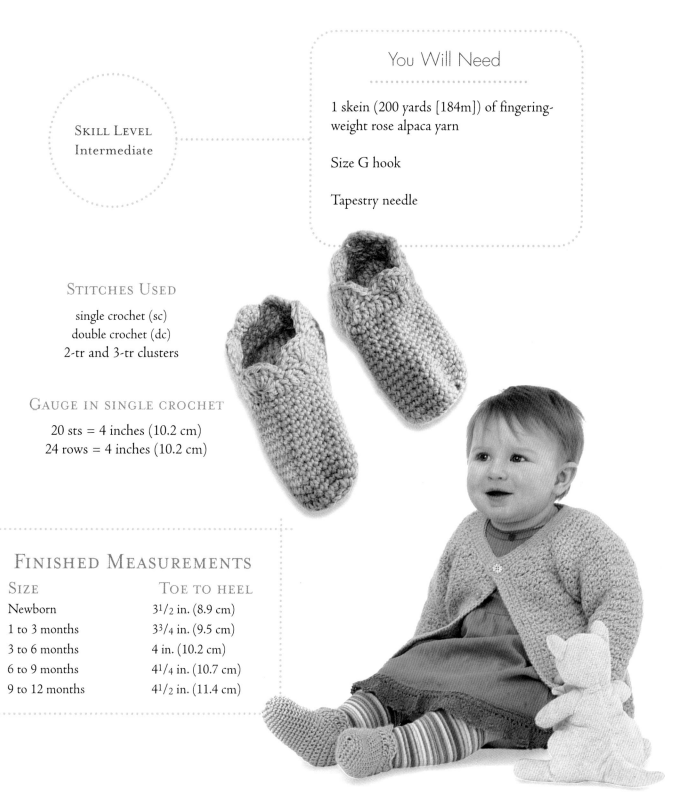

SKILL LEVEL
Intermediate

You Will Need

1 skein (200 yards [184m]) of fingering-weight rose alpaca yarn

Size G hook

Tapestry needle

STITCHES USED

single crochet (sc)
double crochet (dc)
2-tr and 3-tr clusters

GAUGE IN SINGLE CROCHET

20 sts = 4 inches (10.2 cm)
24 rows = 4 inches (10.2 cm)

FINISHED MEASUREMENTS

SIZE	TOE TO HEEL
Newborn	3 1/2 in. (8.9 cm)
1 to 3 months	3 3/4 in. (9.5 cm)
3 to 6 months	4 in. (10.2 cm)
6 to 9 months	4 1/4 in. (10.7 cm)
9 to 12 months	4 1/2 in. (11.4 cm)

PATTERN NOTES

Use two strands of yarn held together as one throughout.

See the Specialty Stitches section on page 10 for instructions on making the triple-crochet clusters for the heels.

Toe

Foundation: Ch 4 (4, 5, 5, 6).

Round 1: Ch 1, sc in back half of 2nd ch from hk and back half of next 2 (2, 3, 3, 4) ch, 5 sc in back half of last ch, sc in other half of next 2 (2, 3, 3, 4) ch, 4 sc in last ch, do not turn, 14 (14, 16, 16, 18) sts.

Round 2: Sc in next 4 (4, 5, 5, 6) sts, 2 sc in next 3 sts, sc in next 4 (4, 5, 5, 6) sts, 2 sc in next 3 sts 20 (20, 22, 22, 24) sts.

Rounds 3 to 14: Sc in ea st.

Round 15: Sc in the first 2 sts of the round, turn.

Bottom of Heel

Rows 1 to 8: Ch 1, sc in next 15 (15, 16, 16, 17) sts, turn.

Back of Heel

Sk next 3 sts, dc in next st, 2-(2, 3, 3, 3) tr cluster in next 2 (2, 3, 3, 3) sts, 3-(3, 2, 2, 3) tr cluster in next 3 (3, 2, 2, 3) sts, 2-(2, 3, 3, 3) tr cluster in next 2 (2, 3, 3, 3) sts, dc in next st, sk 2 sts, sl st in last st, turn.

Ankle Edging

Row 1: Ch 3, 24 (24, 28, 28, 32) dc around ankle opening, join beg to end with a sl st, do not turn.

Row 2: [Sk 1 st, 6 dc in next st, sk 1 st, sc in next st] 6 (6, 7, 7, 8) times.

Weave in end.

Repeat the instructions to make the 2nd bootie.

The sample project was made in size 9 to 12 months, using 1 skein (200 yards [184m]) of Jaeger Alpaca 4-ply weight 1¾ ounce (50g) fingering-weight yarn (100% alpaca) in "Down" #384.

LITTLE BOY BLUE ONESIE
and Booties

A onesie is a staple of a baby's wardrobe, but this one is a step up from the three-to-a-package variety. Make it in cool cotton for summer or wool for winter. Add the blue booties on page 80 for a perfectly charming ensemble.

GAUGE IN PATTERN REPEAT

12 patt repeats = 4 inches (10.2 cm)
22 rows = 4 inches (10.2 cm)

You Will Need

STITCHES USED

single crochet (sc)

2 or 3 skeins (each 131 yards [120m]) of DK-weight yarn in light blue*

Size G hook

Tapestry needle

Snap tape or sew-on snaps for closure

1/2 yard (6 mm) of decorative ribbon

Sewing needle and thread to match snap tape or ribbon

1 yard (91.44 cm) medium-weight elastic cord in color to match yarn

*Amount is dependent on size of garment

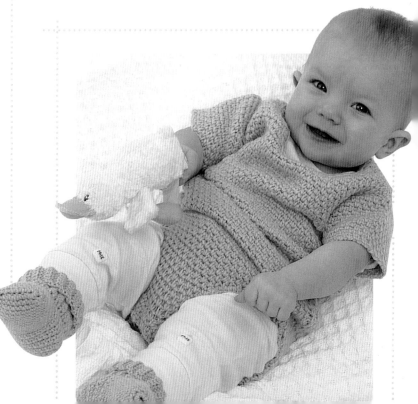

Pattern Notes

In this patt, the ch 2 at the beg of the row is counted as a ch sp on the next row. Patt rep: [Ch 1, sc] in ch sp. To work the patt even without increases or decreases, always finish the row with a (ch1, sc) in the ch 2 sp (the turning ch) at the end of the row.

To increase one patt repeat at the beginning of the row: Ch 3, sc in 3rd ch from hk, continue in patt across the row.

To decrease 1 patt repeat at the beginning of the row: Ch 2, sk 1st ch sp, sc in next ch sp, continue in patt across the row.

To decrease 1 patt repeat at the end of the row: Work in patt to the last ch sp, turn.

Back (beg at crotch–snap closure)

Note: Rows 1 to 4 start the snap section; the pattern seen in the onesie starts on row 5.

Foundation: Ch 9 (9, 11, 11,13), turn.

Row 1: Ch 1, sc in 2nd ch from hk and ea ch across, turn (9, 9, 11, 11, 13 sts).

Rows 2 to 4: Ch 1, sc in each st across, turn.

Row 5: Ch 2, sk 1 sc, [ch 1, sk 1, sc] repeat across, turn (5, 5, 6, 6, 7 total patt reps).

Row 6: Ch 3, sc in 3rd ch from hk [ch 1, sc in ch sp] repeat across.

Rows 7 to 18 (21, 22, 23, 24): Continue in patt increasing 1 patt rep at the beg of ea row (18, 21, 23, 24, 26 total patt reps).

Inc 2 patt reps at the beg of the next 2 rows. To do this, ch 5, sc in 3rd ch from hk, ch 1, sk 1, sc, continue in patt across, turn (22, 25, 27, 28, 30 total patt reps).

Work even in patt until piece measures
5 1/2 inches (13.97 cm) (6 inches [15.24 cm],
6 1/2 inches [16.51 cm], 7 inches [17.7 cm],
7 1/2 inches [19 cm]) from row 22 (24, 26,
28, 28).

Armholes

Dec 2 patt rep at the end of the
next 2 rows, then, dec 1 patt rep
at the beginning of the next
2 rows (16, 19, 21, 22, 24
total patt reps).

Work even for 6 (7, 8, 9, 9)
rows.

Neck and Shoulders
(starting at back)

Work 2 rows even.

To begin the 1st shoulder,
work 6 (6, 7, 7, 8) patt reps
on the next row, turn.

Dec 1 patt rep at the beg of the
row, every other row, at the neck
edge on the next 4 rows (4, 4, 5, 5, 6 patt
reps remaining).

Dec 1 patt rep at the armhole edge on the
next 1 (1, 2, 2, 2) rows (3, 3, 3, 3, 4 patt
reps remaining).

Weave in end.

Work the same for the other side of the neck
and shoulder.

Number of patt reps not worked at center
when you begin working shoulders separately:
4 (7, 7, 8, 8)

Finished Measurements

Size	Width at waist	Shoulder to snap closure when closed
Newborn	7 in. (17.8 cm)	11$^{1}/_{2}$ in. (29.2 cm)
1 to 3 months	8 in. (20.3 cm)	12 in. (30.5 cm)
3 to 6 months	9 in. (22.9 cm)	13 in. (33 cm)
6 to 9 months	9$^{1}/_{2}$ in. (24.1 cm)	14 in. (35.6 cm)
9 to 12 months	10 in. (25.4 cm)	15 in. (38.1 cm)

Front (beg at the crotch snap closure)

Note: Rows 1 to 4 start the snap section; the pattern seen in the onesie starts on row 5.

Foundation: Ch 9 (9, 11, 11, 13), turn.

Row 1: Ch 1, sc in 2nd ch from hk and ea ch across, turn (9, 9, 11, 11, 13 sts).

Rows 2 to 4: Ch 1, sc in each st across, turn.

Row 5: Ch 2, sk 1 sc, [ch 1, sk 1, sc] repeat across, turn (5, 5, 6, 6, 7 total patt reps).

Rows 6 to 10: Ch 2, sc in ch sp [ch 1, sc in ch sp] repeat across.

Rows 11 to 15 (16, 17, 18, 19): Continue in patt increasing one patt rep at the beg of ea row (10, 11, 13, 14, 16 total patt reps).

At the beg of the next 2 rows, Ch 13 (15, 15, 15, 15), sc in 3rd ch from hk, [ch 1, sk 1, sc] 5 (6, 6, 6, 6) times, continue in patt across, turn (22, 25, 27, 28, 30 total patt reps).

Work even in patt until piece measures 5$^{1}/_{2}$ inches (13.97 cm) (6 inches [15.24 cm], 6$^{1}/_{2}$ inches [16.51 cm], 7 inches [17.7 cm], 7$^{1}/_{2}$ inches [19 cm] from row 20 (22, 24, 26, 26).

Work the armholes the same as for the back.

Work even for 4 (5, 6, 7, 7) rows.

Neck and Shoulders (front)

Work 2 rows even.

To begin one shoulder, work 6 (6, 7, 7, 8) patt reps on the next row, turn.

Dec 1 patt rep at the beg of the row, every other row, at the neck edge on the next 4 rows (4, 4, 5, 5, 6 patt reps remaining).

Work 2 rows even.

Dec 1 patt rep at the armhole edge on the next 1 (1, 2, 2, 2) rows (3, 3, 3, 3, 4 patt reps remaining).

Weave in end.

Work the same for the other side of the neck and shoulder.

Number of patt reps not worked at center when you begin working shoulders separately: 4, (7, 7, 8, 8)

Sleeve (make two)

Foundation: Ch 31 (33, 35, 37, 39), turn.

Row 1: Ch 2, sc in 3rd ch from hk [ch 1, sk 1, sc] repeat across, turn (16, 17, 18, 19, 20 total patt reps).

Continue in patt, increasing one patt rep at the beg of ea row for the next 4 (4, 6, 6, 8) rows (20, 21, 24, 25, 28 total patt reps).

For the next 6 (6, 7, 7, 8) rows, continue in patt decreasing one patt rep at the beg and end of ea row (8, 9, 10, 11, 12 total patt reps).

Weave in end.

Assembly

Sew the shoulder seams tog. Center the sleeve over the shoulder seam and sew in place. Sew the side seams and underarm seams.

Finishing

Sc around the leg openings. Thread 2 strands of elastic through the sc sts along the leg openings and gather slightly.

Chain stitch along the neckline, about 1/2-inch (1.3 mm) from the edge. Sc over the neckline, placing the hook through each chain stitch as you make your stitches.

Weave in end.

Sew snap tape to crotch openings, or to make your own snap tape, cut two strips of decorative ribbon, each 1 inch (2.5 cm) longer than the crotch openings. Fold the ends under 1/2 inch (1.3 cm) and baste ends. Sew snaps to the ribbon, then sew the ribbon to the onesie.

The sample project was made in size 9 to 12 months, using 3 skeins (each 131 yards [120m]) of Jaeger Baby Merino DK-weight 1¾-ounce (50 g) yarn (100% merino wool) in "Powder" #222.

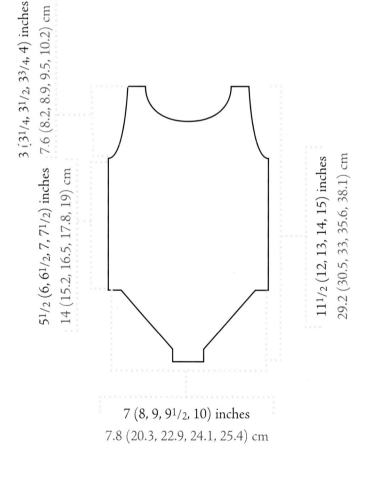

3 (3¼, 3½, 3¾, 4) inches
7.6 (8.2, 8.9, 9.5, 10.2) cm

5½ (6, 6½, 7, 7½) inches
14 (15.2, 16.5, 17.8, 19) cm

11½ (12, 13, 14, 15) inches
29.2 (30.5, 33, 35.6, 38.1) cm

7 (8, 9, 9½, 10) inches
7.8 (20.3, 22.9, 24.1, 25.4) cm

BOOTIES

SKILL LEVEL
Intermediate

STITCHES USED

single crochet (sc)
double crochet (dc)
2-tr and 3-tr clusters

GAUGE IN SINGLE CROCHET

20 sts = 4 inches (10.2 cm)
24 rows = 4 inches (10.2 cm)

FINISHED MEASUREMENTS

SIZE	TOE TO HEEL
Newborn	3$1/2$ in. (8.8 cm)
1 to 3 months	3$3/4$ in. (9.5 cm)
3 to 6 months	4 in. (10.16 cm)
6 to 9 months	4$1/4$ in. (10.7 cm)
9 to 12 months	4$1/2$ in. (11.43 cm)

PATTERN NOTES

See the Specialty Stitches section on page 10 for instructions on the triple-crochet clusters for the heels.

Toe

Foundation: Ch 4 (4, 5, 5, 6).

Round 1: Ch 1, sc in back half of 2nd ch from hk and back half of next 2 (2, 3, 3, 4) ch, 5 sc in back half of last ch, sc in other half of next 2 (2, 3, 3, 4) ch, 4 sc in last ch, do not turn (place marker) (14, 14, 16, 16, 18 sts).

Round 2: Sc in next 4 (4, 5, 5, 6) sts, 2 sc in next 3 sts, sc in next 4 (4, 5, 5, 6) sts, 2 sc in next 3 sts (20, 20, 22, 22, 24 sts).

Rounds 3 to 14: Sc in ea st.

Round 15: Sc in the first 2 sts of the round, turn.

Bottom of Heel (continuing from toe)

Rows 1 to 8: Ch 1, sc in next 15 (15, 16, 16, 17) sts, turn.

Back of Heel

Sk next 3 sts, dc in next st, 2-(2, 3, 3, 3) tr cluster in next 2 (2, 3, 3, 3) sts, 3-(3, 2, 2, 3) tr cluster in next 3 (3, 2, 2, 3) sts, 2-(2, 3, 3, 3) tr cluster in next 2 (2, 3, 3, 3) sts, dc in next st, sk 2 sts, sl st in last st, turn.

Ankle Edging (continuing from the back of the heel)

Row 1: Ch 1, 27 (27, 29, 29, 31) sc around ankle opening, join beg to end with a sl st. Cut yarn to 18 inches (45.72 cm) set aside.

Ribbing

Foundation: Ch 12 (13, 13, 14, 15).

Row 1: Ch 1, sc in 2nd ch from hk and ea ch across, turn (12, 13, 13, 14, 15 sts).

Row 2: Ch 1, sc in the back half of ea st across, turn.

Rows 3 to 14 (14, 14, 16, 16): Repeat row 2.

Cut the yarn to 12 inches (30.48 cm) and weave the first row to the last row, creating a tube.

Assembly

Using the tail at the ankle edging, sew the ribbing to the ankle. Weave in end.

Repeat instructions for 2nd bootie.

The sample project was made in size 9 to 12 months, using 1 skein (131 yards [120m]) of Jaeger Baby Merino DK-weight 1³/₄-ounce (50 g) yarn (100% merino wool) in "Powder" #222.

SOFT-AS-A-CLOUD DRESS

SKILL LEVEL
Intermediate

This sweet long-sleeved dress keeps Baby warm, comfortable, and stylish. Once you're done with the border pattern and the yoke, the rest of the dress is a breeze to make. It's easy to make the pattern longer if necessary before assembly.

You Will Need

3 to 4 skeins (each 200 yards [183m]) of fin-gering-weight yarn in periwinkle*

Size E hook

Tapestry needle

Amount depends on size of garment

GAUGE IN DOUBLE CROCHET

22 sts = 4 inches (10.2 cm)
12 rows = 4 inches (10.2 cm)

STITCHES USED

single crochet (sc)
double crochet (dc)
half-double crochet (hdc)

PATTERN NOTES

The yoke and sleeves are worked from one wrist to the other.

In the yoke and on the sleeves, the chain at the beg of each row does count as a stitch.

In the skirt, the chain at the beg of each round marks the center back.

As you crochet in the round on the skirt, each row of stitches slants to the left. You need to straighten the rows when you block the skirt before assembly.

YOKE AND SLEEVES
First Sleeve (beg at wrist)

Foundation: Ch 27 (30, 33, 35, 38).

Row 1: Ch 3, dc in 4th ch from hk and ea ch across, turn 27 (30, 33, 35, 38) sts.

Rows 2 to 3: Ch 3, dc in ea st across, turn.

Rows 4 to 20: Increase 1 st at beg of ea row (45, 48, 51, 53, 56 sts).

Work even for 0 (2, 4, 5, 6) more rows.

YOKE
First Shoulder

Dec 3 sts at beg and end of row. To do this, ch 1, sl st in 1st 3 sts, ch 3, dc in ea st across to the last 3 sts, turn (39, 42, 45, 47, 50 sts).

Work even for 5 (6, 6, 7, 7) more rows.

Neck

Separate for front and back, working 17 (18, 19, 20, 21) sts for the back and 10 (11, 11, 12, 12) sts for the front, working even in patt for 9 (9, 10, 11, 12) more rows.

FINISHED MEASUREMENTS

SIZE	YOKE WIDTH	SKIRT CIRCUMFERENCE
Newborn	7 in. (17.8 cm)	26 in. (66 cm)
1 to 3 months	8 in. (20.3 cm)	28 in. (71 cm)
3 to 6 months	9 in. (22.9 cm)	30 in. (76.2 cm)
6 to 9 months	9$1/2$ in. (24.1 cm)	31 in. (78.7 cm)
9 to 12 months	10 in. (25.4 cm)	32 in. (81.2 cm)

Next Shoulder

Ch 12 (13, 15, 15, 17) between front and back. Attach a new length of yarn at the back edge and work across the back, 12 (13, 15, 15, 17) ch and the front, joining the front to the back again (39, 42, 45, 47, 50 sts).

Work even for 4 (5, 5, 6, 6) more rows.

Second Sleeve

To increase 3 sts at one end of the 1st row of the sleeve, at the beg of the next row, ch 7 sts, sl st in the 2nd ch from the hk and the next 2 ch. Sk the next 3 ch and dc in ea dc st across to the end of the row.

To increase 3 sts at the beg of the row, ch 7 sts, dc in 4th ch from hk, dc in next 2 ch and ea dc st across the row, dc in 3 sl sts at the end of the row, turn, 3 sts increased at ea end.

Work even for 0 (2, 4, 5, 6) more rows.

Decrease 1 st at beg of the next 17 rows (28, 31, 34, 36, 39 sts).

Work even for 3 more rows. Weave in end.

Skirt length	Sleeve length	Sleeve circumference at wrist
8 1/2 in. (21.6 cm)	8 1/2 in. (21.6 cm)	5 in. (12.7 cm)
9 1/2 in. (24.1 cm)	9 1/2 in. (24.1 cm)	5 1/2 in. (14 cm)
10 1/2 in. (26.7 cm)	10 1/2 in. (26.7 cm)	6 in. (15.2 cm)
11 1/2 in. (29.2 cm)	11 in. (27.9 cm)	6 1/2 in. (16.5 cm)
12 1/2 in. (31.8 cm)	11 1/2 in. (29.2 cm)	7 in. (17.8 cm)

Skirt *(beg at the bottom)*

Foundation: Ch 132 (138, 150, 156, 162).

Row 1: Ch 3, dc in 4th ch from hk and ea ch across, sl st in top of ch 3 to join into a circle.

Row 2: Ch 4, sk 2 sts, 3 dc in next st (this is a 3-dc shell) [ch 1, sk 2 sts, 1 dc in next st, ch 1, sk 2 sts, 3 dc in next st (3-dc shell)] repeat to 3rd st from end, ch 1, sl st to 3rd ch in ch 4.

Row 3: Sl st in 1st 2 sts, ch 3, 1 dc in same st, [dc, ch1, dc] in next st, 2 dc in next st *working in the next 3-dc shell: 2 dc in 1st st, [dc, ch1, dc] in next st, 2 dc in last st* repeat between * * for all shells, sl st in top of ch 3.

Row 4: Ch 3, [6 dc in ch-1 sp, 1 dc in sp between shells] repeat around, ending with 6 dc, then sl st in top of ch 3.

Row 5: Ch 3, [dc in 1st 2 sts of 6-dc shell, hdc in next two sts of shell, dc in last two sts of shell, sk 1 st to get to next shell] repeat around, sl st in top of ch 3 (132, 138, 150, 156, 162 sts) and one step-up ch.

Row 6: Ch 3, dc between 1st and 2nd st, and between the next 4 sts [sk next st, 5 dc between ea of next 5 sts] repeat around, sl st in top of ch 3, 110 (115, 125, 130, 135) sts and 1 step-up ch.

Row 7: Ch 3, dc between ch 3 and 1st st, dc between ea st around except the last sp between the last st and the ch 3, sl st in top of ch 3.

Repeat row 7 until skirt measures 8½ inches (21.6 cm) (9½ inches [24.1 cm], 10½ inches [26.7 cm], 11½ inches [29.2 cm], 12½ inches [31.8 cm]).

Assembly

Block the skirt so the center back is straight.

Fold the yoke and sleeve section in half lengthwise along shoulder line (see diagram on page 87) and sew sleeve seams.

Using a doubled strand of yarn, chain stitch on top of the yoke between the 2nd and 3rd st along the edge of the front and back. Line up the center back of the skirt with the center back of the yoke. Stitch the skirt to the yoke along the inside of the chain stitching, gathering the skirt through the center front and back beginning about 1 inch (2.5 cm) from each side. Stitch the skirt to the edge of the armhole about 1 inch (2.5 cm) on either side of the yoke without gathering. Weave in end.

The sample project was made in size 9 to 12 months, using 4 skeins (each 200 yards [183m]) of Jaeger Matchmaker Merino 4-ply 1¾ ounce (50 g) yarn (100% merino wool) in Opal # 717.

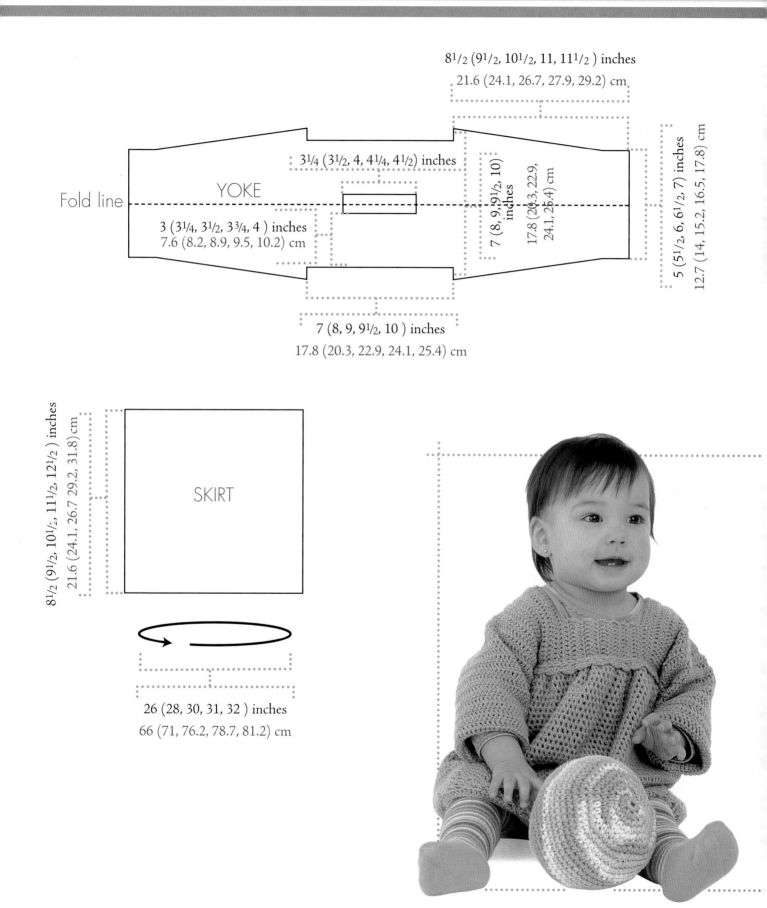

8¹/₂ (9¹/₂, 10¹/₂, 11, 11¹/₂) inches
21.6 (24.1, 26.7, 27.9, 29.2) cm

Fold line

YOKE

3¹/₄ (3¹/₂, 4, 4¹/₄, 4¹/₂) inches

3 (3¹/₄, 3¹/₂, 3³/₄, 4) inches
7.6 (8.2, 8.9, 9.5, 10.2) cm

7 (8, 9, 9¹/₂, 10) inches
17.8 (20.3, 22.9, 24.1, 25.4) cm

5 (5¹/₂, 6, 6¹/₂, 7) inches
12.7 (14, 15.2, 16.5, 17.8) cm

7 (8, 9, 9¹/₂, 10) inches
17.8 (20.3, 22.9, 24.1, 25.4) cm

SKIRT

8¹/₂ (9¹/₂, 10¹/₂, 11¹/₂, 12¹/₂) inches
21.6 (24.1, 26.7 29.2, 31.8) cm

26 (28, 30, 31, 32) inches
66 (71, 76.2, 78.7, 81.2) cm

STRIPED T-SHIRT

A striped t-shirt is a summer classic. The fresh, cool colors of this one make it especially appealing for a baby boy. Change the colors or size of the stripes for variety.

You Will Need

1 to 2 skeins (each 125 yards [115m]) of fingering-weight cotton yarn* in each of the following colors: blue, green, and white

Size E hook

Tapestry needle

Snaps or snap tape

The cotton yarn used for the sample shirt creates a very firm garment. If you want to make an outfit with a little more stretch, try a fingering weight sock yarn or a stretchy yarn such as the one used for the Hooded Lounger or the Soft-as-a-Cloud dress.

GAUGE IN SINGLE CROCHET

20 sts = 4 inches (10.2 cm)
24 rows = 4 inches (10.2 cm)

STITCHES USED

single crochet (sc)

FINISHED MEASUREMENTS

SIZE	WIDTH	LENGTH
Newborn	8 in. (20.3 cm)	10 in. (25.4 cm)
1 to 3 months	9 in. (22.8 cm)	10$^1/_2$ in. (26.6 cm)
3 to 6 months	10 in. (25.4 cm)	11 in. (27.9 cm)
6 to 9 months	10$^1/_2$ in. (26.6 cm)	11 in. (27.9 cm)
9 to 12 months	11 in. (27.9 cm)	12 in. (30.4 cm)

Back

Foundation: Using the blue yarn, ch 40 (46, 50, 54, 56) sts.

Row 1: Ch 1, sc in 2nd ch from hk and ea ch across, turn.

Row 2: Ch 1, sc in ea st across, turn.

Change to the white yarn.

Rows 3 to 4: Ch 1, sc in ea st across, turn.

Repeat row 2 in the following color sequence:

Row 5: Green

Row 6: White

Row 7: Blue

Row 8: Green

Row 9: Blue

Row 10: White

Row 11: Green

Rows 12 to 13: White

Rows 14 to 17: Blue

Repeat the color patt from row 3 to row 17 until the piece measures 10 inches (25.4 cm) (10$^1/_2$ inches [26.6 cm], 11 inches [27.9 cm], 11 inches [27.9 cm], 12 inches [30.4 cm]) long.

Neckline

Mark the 6 (8, 10, 12, 12) center sts and working ea shoulder separately, beg at the marker, dec one st at neckline on the next three rows, continuing in the color patt.

Weave in end.

Front

Work the same as for the back until the front measures 9$^1/_2$ inches (24.1 cm) (10 inches [25.4 cm], 10$^1/_2$ inches [26.6 cm], 10$^1/_2$ inches [26.6 cm], 11$^1/_2$ inches [29.1 cm]) long. Work the neckline the same except, after dec for neckline continue working even in color patt for $^1/_2$-inch (1.3 cm) longer.

Sleeve (make two)
(beg at the bottom of the sleeve)

Foundation: Using the blue yarn, ch 32 (34, 38, 38, 40), turn.

Row 1: Ch 1, sc in 2nd ch from hk and ea ch across, making 2 sc in the last ch, turn (33, 35, 39, 39, 41 sts).

Row 2: Change to the green yarn. Ch 1, sc in ea st across, sc in ch 1 at end of row, turn (one st increased).

Row 3: Repeat row 2 using white yarn.

Rows 4 to 6: Repeat row 2 using the same color sequence as row 1 to 3 (38, 40, 44, 44, 46 total sts).

Rows 7 to 9: Work even, repeating the blue, green, white color sequence.

Rows 10 to 12: Work even in blue.

Weave in ends.

Plackets and Neckline

Attach the green yarn to the top of the left corner of the back. Make 4 rows of sc. Weave in end. Repeat for the front.

Sew the right shoulder seam.

Using the green yarn sc around the neckline.

Weave in end.

Assembly

Place the front placket band over the back placket band. Center the sleeve over the placket and sew the sleeve to the front and back. Sew the sleeve seams and the side seams. Sew snaps to the placket bands.

The sample project was made in size 1 to 3 months, using 1 skein (125 yards [115m]) each of Rowan Cotton Glace 13/4 ounce (50g) yarn (100% cotton) in "Sky" #749, "Mint" #748, and "Bleached" #726.

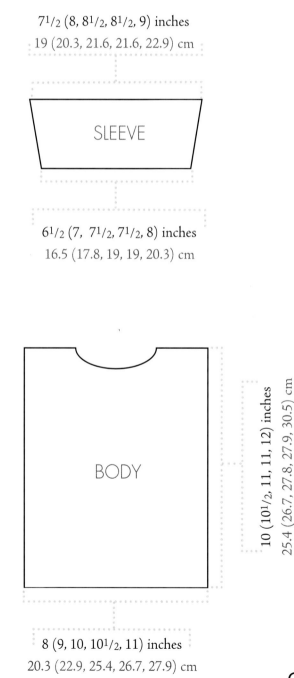

7½ (8, 8½, 8½, 9) inches
19 (20.3, 21.6, 21.6, 22.9) cm

SLEEVE

6½ (7, 7½, 7½, 8) inches
16.5 (17.8, 19, 19, 20.3) cm

BODY

10 (10½, 11, 11, 12) inches
25.4 (26.7, 27.8, 27.9, 30.5) cm

8 (9, 10, 10½, 11) inches
20.3 (22.9, 25.4, 26.7, 27.9) cm

WINTER WONDERLAND CABLE HAT
and Sweater

When you're ready to bundle Baby up for a winter excursion, start with a nice warm hat. For this project, you'll use a front post double crochet stitch and make cables in chain stitch embroidery. Once you've got the hang of the stitches, try making the sweater on page 97.

GAUGE IN SINGLE CROCHET

20 sts = 4 inches (10.2 cm)
24 rows = 4 inches (10.2 cm)

STITCHES USED

single crochet (sc)
front-post double crochet (fpdc)

You Will Need

1 to 2 skeins (each 131 yards [120m])
of DK-weight yarn in off-white

Size G hook

Tapestry needle

Stitch marker

FINISHED MEASUREMENTS

SIZE	CIRCUMFERENCE
Newborn	14 in. (35.5 cm)
1 to 3 months	15 in. (38.1 cm)
3 to 6 months	16 in. (40.6 cm)
6 to 12 months	17 in. (43.1 cm)

Since the hat will stretch, 6 to 9 and 9 to 12 month-sizes were combined instead of separated as usual.

PATTERN NOTES

You can work the chain stitch cable pattern in one of two ways. You can use your crochet hook and make slip stitches over the finished crochetwork, holding the yarn on the back side of the work and pulling it to the front with the crochet hook, or you can embroider chain stitches using a large tapestry needle.

Ribbing

Foundation: Ch 18 +1

Row 1: Sc in the back half of 2nd ch from hk and ea ch across, turn.

Rows 2 to 68 (to 74, 78, 84): Ch 1, sc in the back half of ea st, turn.

Row 69 (75, 79, 85): To join the ribbing into a tube, ch 1, [push the hk through the back half of the next st and through both halves of the 1st st in the foundation ch, make a sl st], repeat for ea st across. Do not turn.

Body of Hat

Row 1: Ch 1, 69 (75, 79, 85) sc along top edge of ribbing, sl st into ch 1 to join tog, place marker. Sl st counts as st in round (70, 76, 80, 86 sts).

Round 2 for size Newborn: [Fpdc, 5 sc, fpdc, 9sc] 4 times, fpdc, 5 sc.

Round 2 for size 1 to 3 months: Fpdc, 9 sc, [fpdc, 5 sc, fpdc, 9sc] 4 times, 2 sc.

Round 2 for size 3 to 6 months: Fpdc, 9 sc, [fpdc, 5 sc, fpdc, 9sc] 4 times, fpdc, 5 sc.

CABLE HAT CHART

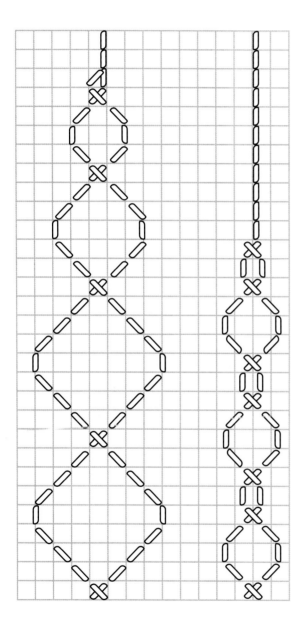

Round 2 for size 6 to 12 months: [Fpdc, 5 sc, fpdc, 9sc] 5 times, fpdc, 5 sc.

Rounds 3 to 12: Fpdc in all fpdc and sc in all sc.

Round 13: Continue in patt, decreasing one st on either side of ea fpdc.

Rounds 14 to 19: Work in patt.

Round 20: Repeat round 13.

Rounds 21 to 23: Work in patt.

Round 24: Continue in patt, decreasing one sc next to the fpdc in the 5-st sc sections.

Rounds 25 to 26: Work in patt.

Round 27: Continue in patt, decreasing 2 sc in ea of the 3-st sc sections.

Rounds 28 to 29: Work in patt.

Round 30: Ch 2, fpdc in all fpdc, sk all sc, join to top of ch 2 with sl st.

Round 31: Ch 3, fpdc in all sts around, join to top of ch 3 with sl st. Weave in end.

Chain stitch the cable pattern as shown in the hat chart, using two 1¹/₂ yard (1.3 m) strands of yarn held tog as one decreasing the pattern as the hat narrows near the top. You will need to have both sections of the cables in progress at once so you can alternatively overlap the chain stitch as you work. Weave in end.

Cut the remaining yarn into 6-inch (15.2 cm) lengths gathered in groups of six or eight strand bunches. Fold ea bunch in half and attach it with a sl st between the sts in the last row of fpdc at the top of the hat.

Fold up ribbing.

The sample project was made for size 9 to 12 months, using 2 skeins (each 131 yards [120m]) of Jaeger Baby Merino DK-weight 1³/₄ ounce (50 g) yarn (100% merino wool) in "Pearl" #203.

WINTER SWEATER WITH CABLES

You Will Need

5 or 6 skeins (each 131 yards [120 m]) of DK-weight yarn in off- white

Size G hook

Tapestry needles

4 buttons, each 1/2-inch (1.3 cm) in diameter

SKILL LEVEL
Intermediate

STITCHES USED

single crochet (sc)
double crochet (dc)
front-post double crochet (fpdc)

GAUGE IN SINGLE CROCHET

20 sts = 4 inches (10.2 cm)
24 rows = 4 inches (10.2 cm)

Finished Measurements

Size	Width	Length
Newborn	9 in. (22.8 cm)	9 in. (22.8 cm)
1 to 3 months	9$^1/_2$ in. (24.1 cm)	9$^1/_2$ in. (24.1 cm)
3 to 6 months	10 in. (25.4 cm)	10 in. (25.4 cm)
6 to 9 months	10$^1/_2$ in. (26.6 cm)	10$^1/_2$ in. (26.6 cm)
9 to 12 months	11 in. (27.9 cm)	11 in. (27.9 cm)

Back
Back Ribbing

Foundation: Ch 6, turn.

Row 1: Ch 1, sc in the back half of 2nd ch from hk and ea ch across, turn.

Rows 2 to 44 (to 48, 50, 52, 54): Ch 1, sc in the back half of ea st, turn.

Row 45 (49, 51, 53, 55): Ch 1, sc in the back half of ea st, do not turn.

Back Body (beg on the wrong side)

Row 1: Ch 1, 45 (49, 51, 53, 55) sc across the long side of the back ribbing, turn.

Row 2: Ch 1, 2 sc, 1 fpdc, 5 (7, 8, 9, 10) sc, 1 fpdc, 1 sc, 2 fpdc, 1 sc, 1 fpdc, 17 sc, 1 fpdc, 1 sc, 2 fpdc, 1 sc, 1 fpdc, 5 (7, 8, 9, 10) sc, 1 fpdc, 2 sc, turn.

Row 3: Ch 1, sc in each st across, turn.

Row 4: Ch 1, 2 sc, 1 fpdc, 5 (7, 8, 9, 10) sc *1 fpdc, 1 sc, sk next st, 1 fpdc in post of next st, 1 fpdc in post of skipped st, 1 sc, 1 fpdc*, 17 sc, repeat between asterisks, 5 (7, 8, 9, 10) sc, 1 fpdc, 2 sc, turn.

Row 5: Ch 1, sc in each st across, turn.

Repeat rows 2 through 5 until piece measures 9 inches (22.8 cm) (9$^1/_2$ inches [24.1 cm], 10 inches [25.4 cm], 10$^1/_2$ inches [26.6 cm], 11 inches [27.9 cm].

Left Placket Band

Row 1: Beg on the wrong side at the right corner, ch 1, sc in the front half of the next 15 (15, 16, 16, 18) sts, turn.

Rows 2 to 4: Ch 1, sc in next 15 (15, 16, 16, 18) sts, turn.

Weave in end.

Right Placket Band

Row 1: Beg on the wrong side, attach yarn in the 16th (16th, 17th, 17th, 19th) st from the left edge on the top row of the Back. Ch 1, sc in the front half of the next 15 (15, 16, 16, 18) sts, turn.

Rows 2 to 4: Ch 1, sc in the next 15 (15, 16, 16, 18) sts, turn.

Weave in end.

Front

Work as for the back less 7 rows before plackets.

Left Front Neckline Shaping
(beg on a right-side row)

Row 1: Ch 1, work 20 (20, 22, 22, 24) sts in patt, turn.

Row 2: Ch 1, sk 2 sts, work to end in patt, turn (18, 18, 20, 20, 22 total sts).

Row 3: Ch 1, work 18 (18, 20, 20, 22) sts in patt, turn.

Row 4: Ch 1, sk 2 sts, work to end in patt, turn (16, 16, 18, 18, 20 total sts).

Row 5: Ch 1, work 15 (15, 16, 16, 18) sts in patt, turn.

Rows 6 to 7: Ch 1, work even in patt, turn.

CABLE SWEATER CHART

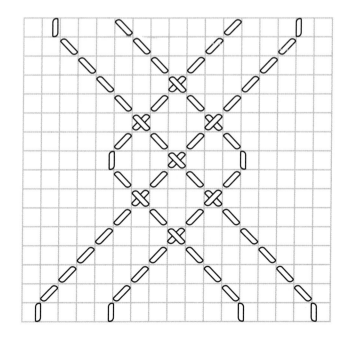

Left Front Buttonhole Placket Band

Row 1: Ch 1, beg on right side, sc in back half of next 15 (15, 16, 16, 18) sts, turn.

Row 2: Ch 1, sc across, turn.

Row 3: Ch 1, 3 (3, 3, 3, 4) sc, ch 2, sk next 2 sts, 4 sc, ch 2, sk next 2 sts, 4 (4, 5, 5, 6) sc, turn.

Row 4: Ch 1, 4 (4, 5, 5, 6) sc, sc in next two ch, 4 sc, sc in next two ch, 3 (3, 3, 3, 4) sc, turn.

Row 5: Ch 1, sc in ea st across.

Weave in end.

Right Front Neckline Shaping
(beg on right-side row)

On a right side row, attach a new length of yarn to the 21st (21st, 23rd, 23rd, 25th) st from the left corner along the top row.

Row 1: Ch 1, work in patt to the end of the row, (20, 20, 22, 22, 24 sts), turn.

Row 2: Ch 1, work in patt for 20 (20, 22, 22, 24) sts, turn.

Row 3: Ch 1, sk 2 sts, work in patt to end of row, turn (18, 18, 20, 20, 22 total sts).

Row 4: Ch 1, work in patt for 18 (18, 20, 20, 22) sts, turn.

Row 5: Ch 1, sk 2 sts, work in patt to end of row, turn (16, 16, 18, 18, 20 total sts).

Row 6: Ch 1, work in patt for 15 (15, 17, 17, 19) sts, turn.

Row 7: Ch 1, work even in patt, turn.

Right Front Buttonhole Placket Band

Row 1: Ch 1, beg on wrong side, sc in the front half of the next 15 (15, 16, 16, 18) sts, turn.

Row 2: Ch 1, sc across, turn.

Row 3: Ch 1, 3 (3, 3, 3, 4) sc, ch 2, sk next 2 sts, 4 sc, ch 2, sk next 2 sts, 4 (4, 5, 5, 6) sc, turn.

Row 4: Ch 1, 4 (4, 5, 5, 6) sc, sc in next two ch, 4 sc, sc in next two ch, 3 (3, 3, 3, 4) sc, turn.

Row 5: Ch 1, sc in ea st across.

Weave in end.

Sleeve (make two)
Sleeve Ribbing

Foundation: Ch 4, turn.

Row 1: Ch 1, sc in the back half of 2nd ch from hk and ea ch across, turn.

Rows 2 to 30 (to 32, 32, 34, 36): Ch 1, sc in the back half of ea st, turn.

Row 31 (33, 33, 35, 37): Ch 1, sc in the back half of ea st, do not turn.

Sleeve Body (beg on the wrong side)

Row 1: Ch 1, 31 (33, 33, 35, 37) sc across the long side of the sleeve ribbing, turn.

Row 2: Ch 1, 10 (11, 11, 12, 13) sc, 1 fpdc, 9 sc, 1 fpdc, 10 (11, 11, 12, 13) sc, turn.

Row 3: Ch 1, sc in each st across, turn.

Rows 4 to 35: Work in patt of rows 2 and 3, increasing 1 st on ea side of the right side row every 4th row 9 times.

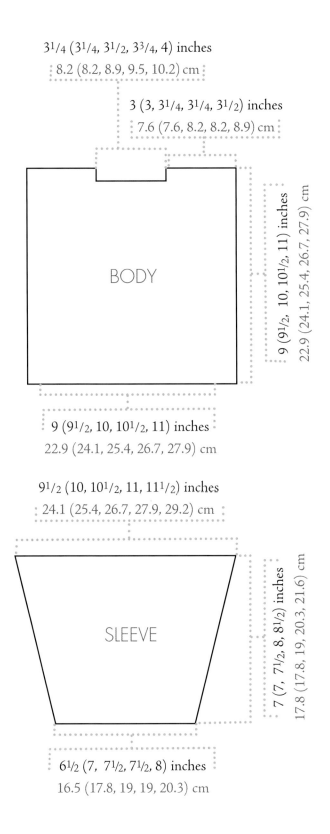

3¼ (3¼, 3½, 3¾, 4) inches
8.2 (8.2, 8.9, 9.5, 10.2) cm

3 (3, 3¼, 3¼, 3½) inches
7.6 (7.6, 8.2, 8.2, 8.9) cm

BODY

9 (9½, 10, 10½, 11) inches
22.9 (24.1, 25.4, 26.7, 27.9) cm

9 (9½, 10, 10½, 11) inches
22.9 (24.1, 25.4, 26.7, 27.9) cm

9½ (10, 10½, 11, 11½) inches
24.1 (25.4, 26.7, 27.9, 29.2) cm

SLEEVE

7 (7, 7½, 8, 8½) inches
17.8 (17.8, 19, 20.3, 21.6) cm

6½ (7, 7½, 7½, 8) inches
16.5 (17.8, 19, 19, 20.3) cm

Work even until sleeve measures 7-inches
(17.8 cm) (7 inches [17.8 cm] 7½ inches
[19 cm], 8 inches [20.3 cm], 8½ inches
[21.6 cm] long. Weave in end.

Embroidery and Finishing

For the cables on the sleeves and on either side
of the center cable on the sweater front, follow
the pattern for the first two diamonds on the
chart for the hat on page 95. For the large center cable follow the pattern repeat on page 99.

Using two strands of yarn held together as one,
make chain stitch cables along the front and
sleeves as shown in the chart. You will need to
have all the cables that overlap in progress at
once so you can alternately overlap the chain
stitch as you work.

Using two strands of yarn held together as one,
sc along the neckline of the front and back.

Weave in end.

Assembly

Overlap the front placket bands over the back
placket bands, and baste armhole top edges.
Center the sleeves over the placket bands and
sew the sleeves to the front and back. Sew the
sleeve and side seams. Sew buttons to the bands
on the back of the sweater.

*The sample project was made in size 6 to 9 months,
using 6 skeins (each 131 yards [120m]) of Jaeger Baby
Merino DK-weight 1¾ ounce (50 g) yarn (100%
merino wool) in "Pearl" #203.*

HOODED JACKET WITH FROG CLOSURE

SKILL LEVEL
Intermediate

*T*his darling jacket is great for layering. Pair it with footed tights like the ones on page 28 for head-to-toe coverage, or add it on over a onesie and pants. The frog closure makes it easy to slip on and off of a baby on the go.

You Will Need

2 to 3 skeins (each 200 yards [183m]) of fingering-weight yarn in teal

Size E hook

Size 8 steel hook

Purchased frog closure or 2 feet (60.9 cm) of 1/8-inch (3 mm) wide rat-tail cord and 1 skein of 6-strand embroidery floss to match or compliment yarn color

Sewing needle and thread

Tapestry needle

GAUGE IN PATTERN

9 patt repeats = 4 inches (10.2 cm)
11 rows = 4 inches (10.2 cm)

STITCHES USED

single crochet (sc)
double crochet (dc)

Right Front (working from side to center or center to side, using size E hook)

Foundation: Ch 54 (60, 66, 69, 72).

Row 1: Ch 3, [dc, ch 1, dc] in 4th ch from hk, (sk 2 ch, [dc, ch 1, dc] in next ch) repeat across to the last 2 ch, dc in last ch, turn (18, 20, 22, 23, 24 patt repeats).

Row 2: Ch 2, ([dc, ch 1, dc] in ch sp) repeat across, dc in top of ch, turn.

Repeat row 2 until piece measures 4 inches (10.2 cm) (4$\frac{1}{2}$ inches [11.4 cm], 5 inches [12.7 cm], 5$\frac{1}{4}$ inches [13.5 cm], 5$\frac{1}{2}$ inches [14 cm]). Weave in end.

Left Front

Make the same as for right front.

Back

Work the same as for right front, repeating row 2 until piece measures 8 inches (20.3 cm) (9 inches [22.9 cm], 10 inches [25.4 cm], 10$\frac{1}{2}$ inches [26.7 cm], 11 inches [27.9 cm]).

Sleeve (make two)

Foundation: Ch 45 (51, 57, 60, 63).

You will have 15 (17, 19, 20, 21) patt repeats.

Work the same as for right front, repeating row 2 until piece measures 6$\frac{1}{2}$ inches (16.5 cm) (7 inches [17.8 cm], 8 inches [20.3 cm], 8$\frac{1}{2}$ inches [21.6 cm], 9 inches [22.9 cm]).

Hood

Foundation: Ch 72 (78, 84, 90, 96).

You will have 24 (26, 28, 30, 32) patt repeats.

Work the same as for right front, repeating row 2 until the piece measures 4$\frac{1}{2}$ inches (11.4 cm) (5 inches [12.7 cm], 5$\frac{3}{4}$ inches [14.6 cm], 6 inches [15.2 cm], 6$\frac{1}{4}$ inches [15.8 cm].

FINISHED MEASUREMENTS

Size	Circumference at chest	Sleeve length (unfolded)	Jacket length (from shoulder seam)
Newborn	16 in. (40.6 cm)	6$\frac{3}{4}$ in. (17.1 cm)	8 in. (20.3 cm)
1 to 3 months	18 in. (45.7 cm)	7$\frac{1}{2}$ in. (19 cm)	9 in. (22.9 cm)
3 to 6 months	20 in. (50. 8 cm)	8$\frac{1}{2}$ in. (21.6 cm)	10 in. (25.4 cm)
6 to 9 months	21 in. (53.3 cm)	9 in. (22.9 cm)	10$\frac{1}{2}$ in. (26.7 cm)
9 to 12 months	22 in. (55.8 cm)	9$\frac{1}{2}$ in. (24.1 cm)	11 in. (27.9 cm)

Assembly

Fold the hood in half lengthwise. Sew one of the long sides together to make the center back of the hood.

Sew the bottom edge of the hood to the top edge of the back piece and front pieces as shown (see figure 1).

Sew the remaining top edge of the back to the remaining top edge of the fronts, creating the shoulder seams.

Center the sleeves over the shoulder seams and sew in place.

Sew the side seams and sleeve seams. Weave in ends.

Turn the sleeves up about 1 inch (2.5 cm) and repeat for a total of 2 inches (5.1 cm).

FIGURE 2

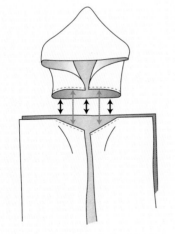

FIGURE 1

LEFT
RIGHT
FRONT

8 (9, 10, 10 1/2, 11) inches
20 (22.9, 25.4, 26.7, 27.9) cm

4 (4 1/2, 5, 5 1/4, 5 1/2) inches
10.2 (11.4, 12.7, 13.3, 14) cm

BACK

8 (9, 10, 10 1/2, 11) inches
20 (22.9, 25.4, 26.7, 27.9) cm

8 (9, 10, 10 1/2, 11) inches
20 (22.9, 25.4, 26.7, 27.9) cm

SLEEVE

6 3/4 (7 1/2, 8 1/2, 9, 9 1/2) inches
17 (19, 21.6, 22.9, 24.1) cm

6 1/2 (7, 8, 8 1/2, 9) inches
16.5 (17.8, 20.3, 21.6, 22.9) cm

HOOD

11 (12, 13, 13 3/4, 14 1/2) inches
27.9 (30.5, 33, 9.5, 36.8) cm

4 1/2 (5, 5 3/4, 6, 6 1/4) inches
11.4 (12.7, 14.6, 15.2, 15.8) cm

To Make the Frog Closure

Using three strands of floss and the size 8 crochet hook, slip stitch over the rat tail cord until you have about 7 inches (17.8 cm) covered with floss. Fold the floss-covered section as shown (see figure 2, page 105) and stitch together in place on the back side so the stitches don't show. Cut the rat tail close to the crochet stitches. Stitch the frog onto the front of the jacket, about 2 inches (5.1 cm) from the neckline.

Make another section of floss covered rat tail that is about 8 1/2-inches (21.6 cm) long. Tie a knot as shown (see figure 3) with the ends, then fold the remaining section as shown. Stitch in place. Cut the rat tail close to the crochet stitches. Stitch the frog on the front of the jacket, opposite the other half.

The sample project was made in size 9 to 12 months, using 3 skeins each 200 yards [183m]) of Jaeger Baby Merino 4-ply 13/4 ounce (50g) fingering-weight yarn (100% merino wool) in Spearmint #118, and 1 skein of DMC six strand 100% cotton floss, color #598.

FIGURE 3

107

WOOLY LAMB
and Turtle

These sweet little stuffed animals are sure to become instant favorites with babies and parents. They're soft and cuddly so they're safe for babies to cuddle or chew on, and the subtle colors are appealing and comforting.

LAMB

GAUGE IN SINGLE CROCHET

20 sts = 4 inches (10.2 cm)
24 rows = 4 inches (10.2 cm)

STITCHES USED

single crochet (sc)
double crochet (dc)

Body

Foundation and Round 1: Using the cream yarn, ch 2, 6 sc in 2nd ch from hk, place marker.

Round 2: 2 sc in ea st around (12 sts).

Round 3: [1 sc, 2 sc] repeat around (18 sts).

Rounds 4 to 6: [sc in sc, 2 sc in between 2-sc increase of previous row] repeat around (24, 30, 36 sts after successive rounds).

Work even in sc for 22 rounds.

Decrease evenly 6 times in ea round, for 4 rounds (12 sts).

Work even for 2 rounds. Cut yarn to 12 inches (30.5 cm). Stuff lightly with fiberfill and set aside.

Head (beg at nose)

Foundation and Round 1: Using the cream yarn, ch 4, 11 dc in 4th ch from hk, place marker.

Round 2: Sc in top of ch-4 sp and in ea st around (12 sts).

Round 3: [sc in next 3 sts, 2 sc in next st] 3 times (15 sts).

Rounds 4 to 12: 2 sc between ea 2-sc increase, sc in all sc sts (18, 21, 24, 27, 30, 33, 36, 39, 42 sts after successive rounds).

Rounds 13 to 14: Work even.

Rounds 15 to 19: Dec 6 times each round evenly spaced around (39, 36, 33, 30, 27 sts after successive rounds).

Stuff head lightly.

Rounds 20 to 21: Dec 6 times each round evenly spaced around (9 sts).

Cut yarn and weave through last round, closing up opening. Weave in end.

Leg and Foot (make four)

Foundation and Round 1: Using the oatmeal yarn, ch 4, 11 dc in 4th ch from hk, place marker.

Round 2 to 3: Sc in ea st around.

Change to cream yarn.

Repeat round 2 ten times. Cut yarn to 12 inches, stuff lightly with fiberfill, and set aside.

Ear (make two)

Foundation and Round 1: Using the oatmeal yarn, ch 4, 11 dc in 4th ch from hk, place marker.

Rounds 2 to 6: Sc in ea stitch around.

Flatten ear and choose a front and back side.

Round 7: Working in patt, dec 1 st on back of ear.

Round 8: Work even.

Rounds 9 to 12: Repeat rounds 7 and 8.

Cut yarn to 12 inches (30.5 cm), press ear flat, and set aside.

Tail

Foundation and Round 1: Using the cream yarn, ch 4, 7 dc in 4th ch from hk, place marker.

Rounds 2 to 5: Sc in ea st around.

Cut yarn to 12 inches (30.5 cm), stuff lightly, and set aside.

Assembly

Using the 12-inch (30.5 cm) tails of yarn, sew the side of the head to the neck. Sew the legs and tail to the body, referring to the photo for placement. Sew the ears to the side of the head.

Wooly Coat

Using oatmeal yarn, sc in a sc on the back of the body. [Ch 12, sc two sts away] repeat all over the back and head.

Face Embroidery

Using 6 strands of embroidery floss, make the nose with buttonhole stitch, covering about 3 dc at the point of the face.

For the eyes, use 12 strands of embroidery floss doubled, and make a French knot for each eye. Take 3 straight stitches, using 6 strands of embroidery floss for the eyelashes.

Be sure to stuff your lamb loosely so that it's soft for Baby.

The sample project was made using 1 skein (131 yards [120m]) Jaeger Extra Fine Merino DK-weight of 1¾ ounce (50g) yarn (100% merino wool) in "Cream" #931, 2 skeins (262 yards [240 m]) in "Oatmeal" # 936, and DMC Cotton Floss #840 for face embroidery.

FINISHED MEASUREMENTS
Approximately 12 inches (30.5 cm) long

TURTLE

You Will Need

1 skein (131 yards [120m]) of DK-weight yarn in each of the following colors: yellow, light green, sage green, and light brown

Size G hook

Tapestry needle

Stitch markers

Polyester fiberfill

Embroidery needle

STITCHES USED

single crochet (sc)
half-double crochet (hdc)
double crochet (dc)
2-st cluster

GAUGE IN SINGLE CROCHET

20 sts = 4 inches (10.2 cm)
24 rows = 4 inches (10.2 cm)

FINISHED MEASUREMENTS

10 inches (25.4 cm) from head to tail

Pentagons for Back (make six)

Foundation and Row 1: Using yellow yarn, ch 2, 10 sc in 2nd ch from hk, sl st into 1st st.

Row 2: Ch 1, ([sc, ch 2, sc] in next st, sc in next st) 5 times, join to ch-1 with a sl st, pulling light green yarn through lp as you make the sl st.

Row 3: Using light green yarn, ch 1, (sc, [sc, ch 2, sc] in next ch sp, sc) 5 times, sl st in 1st st in row, pulling sage green yarn through lp as you make the sl st.

Row 4: Using the sage green yarn, ch 1, (sc, [sc, ch 2, sc] in next ch sp, 2 sc) 5 times, sl st in 1st st in row, pulling brown yarn through lp as you make the sl st.

Row 5: Using the brown yarn, ch 1, (2 sc, [sc, ch 2, sc] in next ch sp, 2 sc) 5 times. Weave in end.

Head (beg at center of face)

Foundation and Round 1: Using the light green yarn, ch 4, 11 dc in 4th ch from hk, place marker.

Round 2: Sc in top of ch-4 and ea st around.

Rounds 3 to 6: Sc in ea st.

Round 7: [Sc, sc 2 tog] repeat around.

Rounds 8 to 12: Sc in ea st.

Weave in end. Stuff lightly with fiberfill and set aside.

Tail

Foundation: Using the light green yarn, Ch 11, turn.

Row 1: Sl st in 2nd ch from hk, sl st, 3 sc, 3 hdc, 2 dc. Weave in end. Set aside.

Foot (make four)

Foundation: Using the light green yarn, ch 4, turn.

Round 1: Sc in the back half of 2nd ch from hk and the back half of next ch, 4 sc in half of last ch, continuing around the other side of the chain, sc in the other half of the next 2 sts, 2 sc in 1st st, place marker.

Rounds 2 to 4: Sc in ea st around.

Round 5: Sc 2 tog at ea side, sc in all other sts.

Rounds 6 to 8: sc in ea st around. Weave in end.

Tummy

Foundation and Round 1: Using the yellow yarn, ch 4, 14 dc in 4th ch from hk, place marker.

Round 2: [Sc in next 2 sts, 2 sc in next st] repeat around.

Round 3 (until piece measures 5 inches [12.7 cm] in diameter): Sc in sc sts, 2 sc between 2-sc shells. Weave in end.

Assembly

For the turtle shell, using the sage green yarn, fasten 2 pentagons tog by making sc sts through the brown sts along one side of the pentagons, inserting the hk through one stitch on ea pentagon, then making the sc so it joins the 2 pieces tog. Weave in end. Repeat for another pentagon until you have the 5 outer pentagons joined into a circle with a pentagon-shaped hole in the middle. Now add the last pentagon to the center in the same manner, working completely around the 6th pentagon, joining all the pentagons to it. Sc around the outer edge of the finished shell.

Baste the tail, legs, and head to the under-side of the shell. Using the sage green yarn, backstitch the shell to the yellow tummy, three-quarters of the way around. Stuff the turtle lightly and continue stitching around. Weave in end.

Face Embroidery

Using the yellow yarn, make 3 or 4 small satin stitches (see page 16) on the head for the turtle eyes, and use stem stitch (see page 16) to make a smile. Weave in end.

The sample project was made using 1 skein (131 yards [120m]) each of Jaeger Matchmaker Merino DK-weight 1¾ ounce (50g) yarn (100% merino wool) in "Butter" #862, "Asparagus" #886, "Sage" #857, and "Soft Camel" #865.

WILD ROSE BLANKET

This sweet blanket will win the hearts of parents and babies alike. The romantic colors are perfect for a baby nursery, but the vine pattern allows you to use your creativity and break out of traditional squares or geometric forms.

GAUGE IN SINGLE CROCHET

13 sts = 4 inches (10.2 cm)
7 rows = 4 inches (10.2 cm)

STITCHES USED

single crochet (sc)
half-double crochet (hdc)
double crochet (dc)
half-triple crochet (htr)
triple crochet (tr)

You Will Need

DK-weight yarn (each skein 200 yards [183m]) in the following amount and colors: 9 skeins of green, 4 skeins of yellow, 2 skeins of pink

Fingering-weight yarn, 2 skeins (each 131 yards [120m]) in light green

Size G hook

Size I hook

Tapestry needle

FINISHED MEASUREMENTS
31 x 36 inches (78.74 x 91.4 cm)

Panel *(make three)*

Use two strands of the sage green yarn held as one throughout.

Foundation: Using the I hk, ch 20, turn.

Row 1: Ch 3, dc in 4th ch from hk and ea ch across, turn (20 dc and one ch 3).

Row 2: Ch 3, dc in ea st across, turn.

Rows 3 to 62: Repeat Row 2.
Weave in end.

Side of Panel

Use two strands of the yellow yarn held together as one throughout.

Attach the yellow yarn to the first row along the side of the green panel.

Row 1: Using the I hk and working along the side edge of the panel, ch 4, [4 dc in end of row, sk one row, 3 dc in the end of the next row, sk one row] repeat along the side of the panel to the last 2 rows, 4 dc in the end of the last row, turn.

Row 2: Ch 3, 1 dc in same st as ch 3, [3 dc between shells, 4 dc between shells] repeat across, 2 dc in last sp, turn.

Row 3: Ch 3, [3 dc between shells, 4 dc between shells] repeat across to last sp between shells, 3 dc in last sp between shells, 1 dc in top of turning ch.

Weave in end.

Repeat for other side of panel.

Embroidery

Using four strands of the pale green yarn held together as one, stem st a vine along the panel. Begin 4 sts from one side on the 2nd row of the panel, and make ea st across two rows vertically. Slant over 1 st, continuing until you reach the st 4 sts from the other side of the panel. Work straight for 3 rows, then begin slanting in the other direction. Continue making this wavy vine all the way until you reach 1 row from the top of the panel. Weave in end. Repeat this for the other 2 panels, working in the same manner but beginning each vine in a different place along the 2nd row of the panel so the vines meander in a different wavy pattern across each panel.

Leaf (make about 36)

Using 3 strands of the light green yarn held together as 1.

Row 1: Using the G hk, ch 4, 3 dc in 4th ch from hk, turn.

Row 2: Ch 3, 1 dc in next 3 sts, dc in 4th ch of ch 4, turn.

Row 3: Ch 3, 5-dc shell, ch 1.

Weave in end.

Rose (make about 27)

(Using one strand of the rose yarn and the G hook)

(Ch 2 [hdc, dc, htr, tr, htr, dc, hdc, ch 1, sl st] in 2nd ch from hk) 5 times. Cut yarn to 8 inches (20.3 cm), tie the beginning and ending tails together, use tails to applique to blanket.

Sew the leaves and flowers along the vines as shown in the sample blanket. Make 3 French knots in the center of each wild rose, using 2 strands of the yellow yarn. Weave in end.

Assembly

Along sides of the panels to be joined, attach the light green yarn, using three strands held together as one. Using the I hk, ch 3, then dc in ea st across. Weave in end.

Hold two panels wrong sides together and attach the rose yarn through the corner of both panels, using two strands held together as one. Using the I hk, sc in ea st across both panels, joining them together. Repeat to join the 3rd panel to complete the blanket. Weave in end.

The sample project was made using Jaeger Baby Merino DK–weight 1¾ ounces (50g) yarn (100% merino wool) in "Buttermilk" #205; Jaeger Matchmaker Merino DK–weight 1¾ ounce (50g) yarn (100% merino wool) in "Sage" # 857 and "Down" #863; and Jaeger Matchmaker Merino 4–Ply weight 1¾ oz (50g) yarn (100% merino wool) in "Croquet" #735.

BASIC BLANKET

Many of the stitch patterns used for baby clothes can be adapted for blankets and pillows. A dress or onesie with a blanket in a matching pattern makes a beautiful gift. This blanket features the same pattern as the Soft-as-a-Cloud Dress on page 82.

SKILL LEVEL
Intermediate

You Will Need

10 skeins (131 yards [120m]) of DK-weight yarn in lavender

Size G hook

Tapestry needle

GAUGE IN DOUBLE CROCHET

20 sts = 4 inches (10.2 cm)
10 rows = 4 inches (10.2 cm)

STITCHES USED

single crochet (sc)
half-double crochet (hdc)
double crochet (dc)

FINISHED MEASUREMENTS
28 x 44 inches (71.1 cm x 1.1 m)

Panel (make two)

Foundation: Ch 36, turn.

Row 1: Ch 3, dc in 4th ch from hook and in ea ch across, turn (36 sts).

Rows 2 to 110: Ch 3, dc in ea st across, turn, except on row 110, do not turn at end of row.

Pattern (along side edge of panel)

Row 1: Continuing along the left side of the panel, ch 3, [3 dc in ch-3 sp, sk one row, 4 dc in next ch-3 sp, sk one row] 27 times, 3 dc in last ch-3 sp, turn.

Row 2: Ch 3, 1 dc in ea st across, 1 dc in top of ch 3, turn.

Row 3: Ch 3, 1 dc [ch 1, sk 2, dc, ch 1, sk 2, 3 dc in next st] 32 times, turn.

Row 4: Ch 3, dc ([dc, ch 1, dc] in next st, 2 dc, sk 3, 2 dc in next st) 32 times [dc, ch 1, dc] in top of ch 3, turn.

Row 5: Ch 3, 3 dc in ch-1 sp, [dc in sp of sk-3 section, 6 dc in ch-1 sp] 32 times, 1 dc in top of ch 3, turn.

Row 6: Ch 3, sk 1, [2 dc, 2 hdc, 2 dc, sk 1] 32 times, 2 dc, 1 hdc, turn.

Row 7: Ch 4, [1 dc between next 2 dc] twice, (sk 1, [1 dc between next 2 dc] twice) 64 times, dc in top of ch 4, turn.

Rows 8 to 11: Ch 4, [dc between sts, ch 1] repeat across, dc in 3rd ch of ch 4, turn.

Weave in end after row 11.

Repeat rows 1 to 10 above on the other side of the panel.

Sew the panels together along row 11. Work row 8 along the top and bottom edge of the blanket.

The sample project was made using 10 skeins (each 131 yards [120m]) of Jaeger Matchmaker Merino DK-weight 1¾-ounce (50g) yarn (100% merino wool) in "Haze" #882.

119

BARGELLO PILLOW
and Tumbling Blocks Blanket

A matching blanket and pillow set makes a great nursery gift that's sure to be cherished for years. It's easy to vary this pattern for different-sized pillows. Vary the order of the colors or add more colors as you like. These are great projects for using up leftover yarn.

GAUGE IN SINGLE CROCHET

16 sts = 4 inches (10.2 cm)
18 rows = 4 inches (10.2 cm)

STITCHES USED

single crochet (sc)
double crochet (dc)
4-st dc cluster

You Will Need

89-yard (82 m) skeins of worsted-weight yarn in the following amounts and colors: 4 skeins yellow, 2 skeins light blue, 2 skeins dark blue

16-inch (40.6 cm) square pillow form

Size H hook

Tapestry needle

Foundation: Using the yellow yarn, ch 144 sts, turn.

Row 1: Ch 3, dc in 4th ch from hk and ea ch across. Do not turn. Being careful not to twist the piece, join the end to the beginning with a sl st. This will mark your side seam.

Row 2: Ch 3, 10 dc, [2 dc, ch 2, 2 dc] in next st, 10 dc, 4-dc cluster in next 4 sts, 5 dc, [2 dc, ch 2, 2 dc] in next st, 5 dc, 4-dc cluster in next 4 sts, join to top of ch-3 with sl st.

Repeat row 2 three more times in yellow, then once in dark blue and once in light blue. Change to yellow. Work the same pattern as row 2, using sc instead of dc throughout. Continue repeating row 2 in the following color sequence: 2 rows in light blue, 1 row in dark blue, 1 row in light blue, 1 row in yellow, 1 sc row in dark blue, 2 rows in

yellow, 1 row in light blue, 2 rows in dark blue, 1 row in yellow, 1 row in dark blue, 1sc row in light blue, 4 rows in yellow. Cut the end to 24 inches (60.9 cm).

Assembly

Turn the pillow cover inside out and backstitch a seam along the top edge using the 24-inch (60.9 cm) tail, stitching straight across the crochetwork to make the pillow top. The points of the zigzags will be at different lengths along the inside seam of the pillow. Turn the pillow right side out and insert the pillow form. Fold the bottom opening of the pillow to the inside and sew a seam across the bottom. Weave in end.

The sample project was made using Jaeger Baby Merino Aran worsted- weight 1¾ ounce (50 g) yarn (100% merino wool); 4 skeins (each 89 yards [82 m]) of "Glow" #762, 2 skeins of "Ice" #770, and 2 skeins of "Eucalyptus" #754

TUMBLING BLOCKS BLANKET

Skill Level
Intermediate

You Will Need

Worsted-weight yarn in 89-yard (82 m) skeins in the following amounts and colors: 4 yellow, 5 light blue, and 5 dark blue

Size H hook

Tapestry needle

Stitches Used

single crochet (sc)
double crochet (dc)
3-dc cluster
4-dc cluster

Gauge in single crochet

16 sts = 4 inches (10.2 cm)
18 rows = 4 inches (10.2 cm)

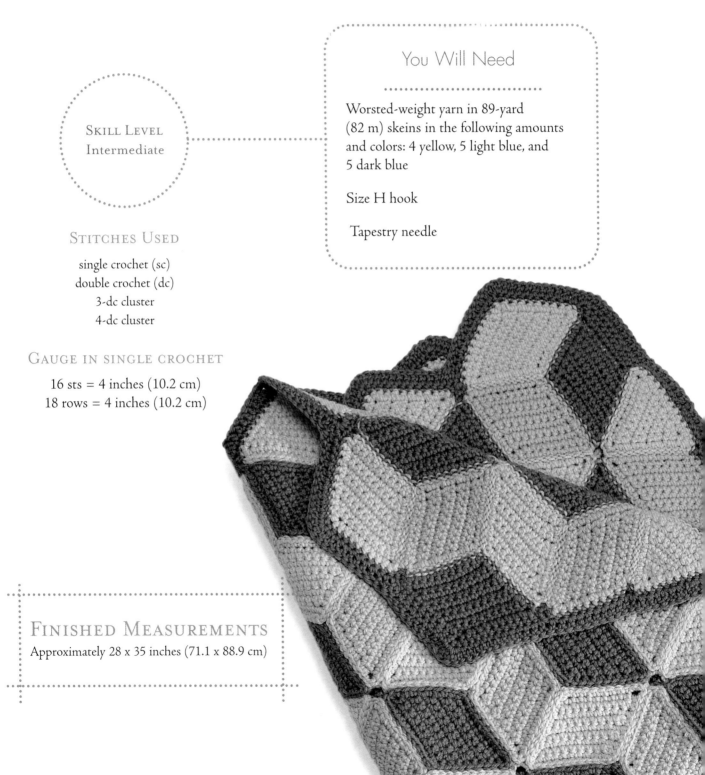

Finished Measurements
Approximately 28 x 35 inches (71.1 x 88.9 cm)

PATTERN NOTES

Decrease stitch (dec 1):

Hk through 1st st, yo, pull through (2 lps on hk).

Hk through 2nd st, yo, pull through (3 lps on hk).

Yo, pull through all (3) lps on hk, (1 lp on hk).

Increase stitch (inc 1): 2 sc in next st.

Rhombus (make 36 in yellow, 35 in dark blue, and 35 in light blue)

Foundation: Ch 10, turn.

Row 1: Ch 1, sc in 2nd ch from hk and ea ch across, turn (10 sts).

Row 2: Ch 1, dec 1, 1 sc in ea of next 7 sts, inc 1, turn.

Row 3: Ch 1, sc in ea st to end, turn (10 sts).

Row 4: Repeat row 2.

Rows 5 to 8: repeat row 3 and row 4.

Edging: Working counter clockwise around the edge of the piece, 1 sc in ea of next 9 sts, 3 sc in last st, 7 sc along side edge, 4 sc in corner, 7 sc along bottom edge (hide tail as you make this side), 3 sc in last st at corner, 7 sc along side edge, 2 sc in corner, 2 sc in 1st st along top edge, 8 sc along top, weave in end.

Triangle (make 6)

Foundation: Ch 10, turn.

Row 1: Ch 1, sc in 2nd ch from hk and ea ch across, turn (10 sts).

Row 2: Ch 1, dec 1, sc in ea st across, turn.

Repeat Row 2 until there is 1 st.

Edging: Working counter clockwise around the edge of the piece, ch 1, 8 sc along left side of triangle, 4 sc in corner, 8 sc along the bottom edge of the triangle, 4 sc in corner, 8 sc along right side of triangle, 4 sc in top corner, weave in end.

Assembly

Using the light blue yarn, make 32 "blocks" by sewing each rhombus together. Sew all the blocks with the colors in the same order, yellow on top, dark blue on the right or left, and light blue on the opposite side. Arrange the blocks so they fit together as in the photograph and sew all the blocks together, adding the triangles and extra rhombuses to make the blanket.

Edging of Blanket

Using the dark blue yarn, sc along the edge of the blanket making 3 sc in the points and a 4-dc cluster in the indentations between the yellow rhombuses. Join the 1st st to the last with a sl st. Ch 3, dc along the edge, making 3 dc in the points and a 3-dc cluster in the 4-dc cluster st and the 2 sts next to the cluster st. Weave in end.

The sample project was made using Jaeger Baby Merino Aran worsted-weight 1¾ ounce (50g) yarn (100% merino wool) 4 skeins (each 89 yards [82m]) of "Glow" #762, 5 skeins of "Ice" #770, and 5 skeins of "Eucalyptus" #754.

HEIRLOOM BLANKET

The overall pattern is elegantly simple, but this blanket's real charm is in the details—the pretty silk ribbon threaded through the border. This is a classic gift or project to keep—sure to become a family heirloom.

You Will Need

10 skeins (each 135 yards [125m]) of DK-weight yarn in cream

Size G hook

Tapestry needle

4 yards of 3/8-inch (9.5 mm) wide silk ribbon

Sewing needle and thread to match ribbon color

GAUGE IN PATTERN

8 patt repeats = 4 inches (10.2 cm)
11 rows = 4 inches (10.2 cm)

STITCHES USED

single crochet (sc)
double crochet (dc)

FINISHED MEASUREMENTS

Approximately 30 x 41 inches (76.2 x 104.1 cm)

Blanket

Foundation: Ch 168

Row 1: Ch 3, [dc, ch 1, dc] in 4th ch from hk, (sk 2 ch [dc, ch 1, dc] in next ch) repeat across, dc in last ch, turn (56 patt repeats).

Row 2: Ch 2 ([dc, ch 1, dc] in ch sp) repeat across, dc in last ch, turn.

Repeat row 2 until the blanket measures 38 inches (96.5 cm). After the last row, do not turn or cut yarn.

Border

Row 1: Continuing counter clockwise around the left top corner of blanket, ch 3, 4 dc in corner, 2 dc in the end of ea row along the left side of the blanket to the next corner, 7 dc in corner, [2 dc in ch-2 sp, 3 dc in next ch-2 sp] repeat along the bottom of the blanket to the next corner ending with 2 dc in last ch-2 sp, 7 dc in 1st row at the bottom right corner, 2 dc in end of ea row along the right side of the blanket to the top right corner, 7 dc in corner, [2 dc in ch sp, 3 dc in next ch sp] repeat across the top of the blanket, sl st in top of ch 3 to join to beg of row. Do not turn.

Row 2: Ch 4, dc in next st [ch 1, dc in next st] 4 times (part of corner), ([ch 1, sk1, dc in next st] repeat along the left side to the next corner, [ch 1, dc in next st] 7 times [bottom left corner]). Repeat for the next 2 sides and corners, [ch 1, sk 1, dc in next st] along the top edge to the last st, ch 1, dc in next st, ch 1, join to 3rd ch in ch 4.

Row 3: [Sk ch sp, 3 dc in next ch sp, ch 4, sl st in top of last dc, 3 dc in same ch sp, sk ch sp, sc in next ch sp] repeat around the blanket. Weave in end.

Adding the Ribbon

Press the ribbon. Thread the large tapestry needle with the ribbon and weave the ribbon in and out of row 2 of the border pattern being careful to keep it from twisting. Bring the ribbon end to the back when the tail is less than 3 inches (7.6 cm). Begin another strip of ribbon where the first one ends. After you have threaded the ribbon around the blanket, turn the blanket over and sew the ribbon pieces together so the seams are behind the crochetwork. Trim the ends to about 1/4 inch (6 mm), turn the raw edge under, and blind hem the ribbon in place.

The sample project was made using 10 skeins (each 135 yards [125m]) of Jaeger Matchmaker Merino 1 3/4 ounce (50g) DK-weight yarn (100% merino wool) in #662 "Cream".

ACKNOWLEDGMENTS

Thank you Joanne O'Sullivan, my editor, for all your work in getting this book together, especially when working out the overall concept of the book at the beginning stages of planning, and of course during the crunch that always happens near the end. Thank you also to Marilyn Hastings for your technical editing of these crochet instructions. Your thorough eye for details has been invaluable.

Thanks also to Dana Irwin and Sandra Stambaugh for adorable photogrpahy, and to Key Associates Design for their beautiful work

Thank you June and Joelle at Westminster Fibers for your help with all the yarn gathering for these projects, especially in the middle of moving facilities.

Finally, thanks to all the babies and their parents for making the book so irresistably cute!

SUPPLY SOURCES

All of the projects in this book (with the exception of the variegated balls) were made with Jaeger or Rowan yarns, distributed in the US by Westminster Yarns. To find a stockist near you, look them up on the web at www.wfibers.com or www.knitrowan.com.

INDEX